Vocabulary
FOR CIVIL
SERVICE TESTS

Vocabulary

FOR CIVIL
SERVICE TESTS

Marguerite Hartill

LEARNINGEXPRESS ®

NEW YORK

Library of Congress Cataloging-in-Publication Data:
Hartill, Marguerite.
   Vocabulary for civil service tests / Marguerite Hartill.—1st ed.
        p. cm.
   ISBN 1-57685-474-4 (pbk.)
      1. Civil service—United States—Examinations—Study guides.
      2. Vocabulary tests—study guides. I. Title.
   JK716.H3532 2003
   351.73'076—dc21

                                                     2003013197

Printed in the United States of America

9 8 7 6 5 4 3 2 1

First Edition

ISBN 1-57685-474-4

For more information or to place an order, contact LearningExpress at:
   55 Broadway
   8th Floor
   New York, NY 10006

Or visit us at:
   www.learnatest.com

Contents

Introduction

Choosing a career as a government employee can be very rewarding. But before you begin your job, you will find that you must take a Civil Service exam. Generally, a Civil Service exam will be comprised of many different sections. Depending on your job field, the type of test you will take may include any or all of the following topics: math, judgment, map reading, number and letter recall, reading tables and graphs, and vocabulary. Vocabulary is a broad topic, and it forms the foundation for reading comprehension, grammar, and spelling. In general, the better your basic vocabulary skills are, the better you will do on the entire test. Civil Service exams require that candidates score well on all parts of the exam, so use the exercises and practice tests in this book to get a feel for the vocabulary topics you will face on the real exam.

▶ HOW TO USE THIS BOOK

Whether your exam is months away or coming up in a few weeks, this book will help you prepare. You should carefully read this introduction and Chapter 1—the LearningExpress Test Preparation System—so you can grasp effective strategies and learn to budget your preparation time wisely. Chapter 1 presents a 30-Day Study Plan and a 14-Day Study Plan. You can decide which of these plans is right for you, or you can create a more personalized plan. Remember to stick as closely as you can to your plan. Always keep your end goal in mind. If you study hard the first time, chances are you will not have to take this exam again—ever!

Once you have set a study plan for yourself, look at the table of contents to see the types of verbal topics covered in this book. The book is organized in six sections: Commonly Tested Words, Vocabulary in Context, Synonyms and Antonyms, Reading Comprehension, Grammar, and Spelling. The structure divides common language arts strands into compact parts so that you can work on each concept and gain mastery. You may want to answer the questions in sequence, or you may decide to study the sections that give you the most difficulty early on in your test preparation.

A helpful 500-word vocabulary list of commonly tested words can be found in Chapter 2. In addition, you may want to have a dictionary or thesaurus handy as you work through the questions in each section. This can help expand your bank of vocabulary words. Another helpful list—entitled Prefixes, Suffixes, and Word Roots—is also included in Chapter 2. Understanding the parts that make up a word can give you a clue about a word's definition, and this can help you make educated guesses when taking your exam.

As you answer the hundreds of practice questions in this book, you will want to check your answers against the answer explanation section at the end of each chapter. If, after answering all the questions in a section, you feel you need more practice, reread the questions and try your hand at responding one more time. Repetition is often the key to success. Studies show that most repetitive tasks become part of a person's inventory of skills over time.

And, finally, there are two practice tests at the end of the book. These exams will give you the chance to measure what you have learned and review any problem areas that you find. If at some point you feel you need further practice or more explanation about vocabulary, you can find it in these Learning-Express publications:

▶ *501 Grammar and Writing Questions*
▶ *501 Synonym and Antonym Questions*
▶ *501 Reading Comprehension Questions, 2nd edition*
▶ *501 Word Analogy Questions*
▶ *Goof-Proof Grammar*
▶ *Goof-Proof Spelling*
▶ *Vocabulary and Spelling Success in 20 Minutes a Day, 3rd edition*

▶ KINDS OF CIVIL SERVICE JOBS

Civil Service jobs range from clerical work to forestry, from social work to cartography, from painting to nursing. The government workforce is diverse with career possibilities in a wide array of specialties and fields, including:

- ▶ Accounting
- ▶ Administration
- ▶ Agriculture
- ▶ Air Traffic Control
- ▶ Biology
- ▶ Budgetary Work
- ▶ Cartography
- ▶ Chemistry
- ▶ Claims Work
- ▶ Clerical Work
- ▶ Conservation
- ▶ Court Work
- ▶ Custodial Work
- ▶ Defense-Related Work
- ▶ Drafting
- ▶ Educational Service
- ▶ Electrical Work

- ▶ Engineering
- ▶ Finance
- ▶ Firefighting
- ▶ Health Services
- ▶ Human Services
- ▶ Information Technology
- ▶ Law Enforcement
- ▶ Legal
- ▶ Machinist Work
- ▶ Nursing
- ▶ Painting
- ▶ Postal Work
- ▶ Service Work
- ▶ Social Work
- ▶ Treasury Work
- ▶ Visa Examination

▶ EARNINGS AND ADVANCEMENT

The government is the largest employer in the United States. Government jobs are secure, have great holiday and vacation schedules, offer health insurance, and provide paid training for employees. Specific benefits may include: 10 paid holidays a year, 13 to 26 paid vacation days a year, 13 sick days a year, group life insurance, medical and dental benefits, and a government pension plan.

Civilian government employees are grouped by the type of work they do. This is called the *series*. The level of their relative positions (based on difficulty) is called the *grade*. Each grade progresses upward through *steps*. The higher the step, the more money you make. Depending on your prior education, you may enter the government pay scale at different grades. For example, high school graduates may enter at GS-2 ("GS" means "General Schedule"), whereas junior college graduates may enter at GS-4.

BASIC PAY UNDER THE GENERAL SCHEDULE PAY PLAN, 2003

For 2003, basic pay under the General Schedule, or GS, pay plan is as follows:

GS-1	$15,214	GS-6	26,130	GS-11	42,976
GS-2	17,106	GS-7	29,037	GS-12	51,508
GS-3	18,664	GS-8	32,158	GS-13	61,251
GS-4	20,952	GS-9	35,519	GS-14	72,381
GS-5	23,442	GS-10	39,115	GS-15	85,140

Please note that GS pay is adjusted according to your geographic location, so the majority of jobs pay more than the base salary listed above. Locality payments in the continental United States range from 8.64% to 19.04% above base pay. Pay rates outside the continental United States are 10% to 25% higher. Also, certain hard-to-fill jobs, usually in the scientific, technical, and medical fields, may have higher starting salaries. Exact pay information can be found on position vacancy announcements.

Source: United States Office of Personnel Management's USAJOBS website, www.usajobs.opm.gov.

▶ ADDITIONAL RESOURCES

If you feel you need even more verbal skills practice you might want to purchase or borrow the following books:

Agnes, Michael, ed. *Webster's New World Compact School and Office Dictionary.* (New York: Random House, 2002).

Bonet, Diana. *Vocabulary Improvement: Words Made Easy.* (Menlo Park, CA: Crisp Publications, 1992).

Contemporary's Word Power. (Lincolnwood, IL: Contemporary Books, 1997).

Krevisky, Joseph, et al. *Random House Webster's Pocket Bad Speller's Dictionary.* (New York: Random House, 1998).

Merriam-Webster's Collegiate Dictionary. (Springfield, MA: Merriam-Webster, 2003).

Nadeau, Ray, et al. *Building a Better Vocabulary.* (Lanham, MD: University Press of America, 1997).

O'Connor, Joyce, ed. *Roget's Desk Thesaurus.* (New York: RHR Press, 2001).

Sheehan, Michael. *Word Parts Dictionary.* (Jefferson, NC: McFarland, 2000.)

Sorsby, Claudia. *Spelling 101.* (New York: St. Martin's, 1996).

For more information on starting your career in civil service, check out LearningExpress's *Civil Service Career Starter* (New York: LearningExpress, 2000).

The following is a list of government websites to check for job information and opportunities:

www.black-collegian.com/career/career-reports/federal2002-1st.shtml

www.capitolpublications.com/governmentjobcenter

www.careersingovernment.com/index.cfm?page=jobView&jobID=1305

www.fedjobs.com/howto.htm

www.federaljobs.net

www.usajobs.opm.gov

www.va.gov/jobs/benefits.htm

▶ MAKE THE COMMITMENT

A rich vocabulary gives you a strong advantage in the workplace. When you have an extensive vocabulary, you can write clear descriptions; you can speak more fluently and with more confidence; you can understand more of what you read; and you can read more sophisticated texts. Achieving a good vocabulary does not come without hard work. Take the time now and make the commitment to improve your vocabulary skills for your Civil Service exam.

Vocabulary
FOR CIVIL
SERVICE TESTS

The LearningExpress Test Preparation System

Taking any test can be tough. But don't let the written test scare you! If you prepare ahead of time, you can achieve a top score. The LearningExpress Test Preparation System, developed exclusively for LearningExpress by leading test experts, gives you the discipline and confidence you need to do your best on the exam.

F irst, the bad news: Getting ready for any test takes work! If you plan to obtain any Civil Service position, you will have to score high on your Civil Service exam. This book focuses specifically on the language skills that are tested on the exam. By honing in on these skills, you will take your first step toward achieving the career of your dreams. However, there are all sorts of pitfalls that can prevent you from doing your best on an exam. Here are some obstacles that can stand in the way of your success:

- ▶ being unfamiliar with the format of the exam
- ▶ being paralyzed by test anxiety
- ▶ leaving your preparation to the last minute
- ▶ not preparing at all
- ▶ not knowing vital test-taking skills, such as:
  - ■ how to pace yourself through the exam
  - ■ how to use the process of elimination
  - ■ when to guess

▶ not being in tip-top mental and physical shape
▶ forgetting to eat breakfast and having to take the test on an empty stomach
▶ forgetting a sweater or jacket and shivering through the exam

What's the common denominator in all these test-taking pitfalls? One word: *control.* Who's in control, you or the exam?

Now, the good news: The LearningExpress Test Preparation System puts *you* in control. In just nine easy-to-follow steps, you will learn everything you need to know to make sure that *you* are in charge of your preparation and your performance on the exam. *Other* test-takers may let the test get the better of them; *other* test-takers may be unprepared or out of test-taking shape, but not *you.* You will have taken all the steps you need to take to earn a top score.

Here's how the LearningExpress Test Preparation System works: Nine easy steps lead you through everything you need to know and do to get ready to succeed on your exam. For each of the steps listed below you will find tips and activities to help you prepare for any exam. It is important that you follow the advice and do the activities, or you won't be getting the full benefit of the system. Each step gives you an approximate time estimate.

Step 1: Get Information	30 minutes
Step 2: Conquer Test Anxiety	20 minutes
Step 3: Make a Plan	50 minutes
Step 4: Learn to Manage Your Time	10 minutes
Step 5: Learn to Use the Process of Elimination	20 minutes
Step 6: Know When to Guess	20 minutes
Step 7: Reach Your Peak Performance Zone	10 minutes
Step 8: Get Your Act Together	10 minutes
Step 9: Do It!	10 minutes
Total	**3 hours**

We estimate that working through the entire system will take you approximately three hours, though it is perfectly okay if you work faster or slower than the time estimates allow. If you can take a whole afternoon or evening, you can work through the entire LearningExpress Test Preparation System in one sitting. Otherwise, you can break it up and do just one or two steps a day for the next several days. It's up to you—remember, you are in control.

▶ STEP 1: GET INFORMATION

Time to complete: 30 minutes
Activity: Read the Introduction

Knowledge is power. The first step in the LearningExpress Test Preparation System is finding out everything you can about the types of questions that will be asked on the verbal section of a Civil Service examination. Practicing and studying the exercises in this book will help prepare you for the verbal section of the Civil Service test. If you haven't already done so, stop here and read the Introduction of this book. There, you will learn how to use this book; review general reading comprehension, vocabulary, grammar, and spelling strategies; see an overview of the kinds of Civil Service jobs available; and be presented with a discussion regarding earnings and advancement for civil servants.

Topics that are tested include:

▶ Vocabulary in Context
▶ Reading Comprehension
▶ Synonyms and Antonyms
▶ Grammar
▶ Spelling

After completing the LearningExpress Test Preparation System, you will then begin to apply the test-taking strategies you learn as you work through practice exercises in the above topic areas (Chapters 3 through 7). You can see how well your training paid off in Chapters 8 and 9, where you will take two practice Civil Service verbal examinations.

▶ STEP 2: CONQUER TEST ANXIETY

Time to complete: 20 minutes
Activity: Take the Test Stress Test

Having complete information about the exam is the first step in getting control of the exam. Next, you have to overcome one of the biggest obstacles to test success: test anxiety. Test anxiety not only impairs your performance on the exam itself, but it can even keep you from preparing. In Step 2, you will learn stress management techniques that will help you succeed on your exam. Learn these strategies now and practice them as you work through the exams in this book, so they'll be second nature to you by exam day.

Controlling Test Anxiety

The first thing you need to know is that a little test anxiety is a good thing. Everyone gets nervous before a big exam—and if that nervousness motivates you to prepare thoroughly, so much the better. It's said that Sir Laurence Olivier, one of the foremost British actors of this century, vomited before every performance. His stage fright didn't impair his performance, however; in fact, it probably gave him a little extra edge—just the kind of edge you need to do well, whether on a stage or in an exam room.

On the next page is the LearningExpress *Test Stress Test*. Stop here and answer the questions on that page to find out whether your level of test anxiety is something you should worry about.

Stress Management Before the Test

If you feel your level of anxiety is getting the best of you in the weeks before the test, here is what you need to do to bring the level down:

- ▶ **Get prepared.** There's nothing like knowing what to expect. Being prepared will put you in control of test anxiety. That's why you are reading this book. Use it faithfully, and remind yourself that you are better prepared than most of the people taking the test.
- ▶ **Practice self-confidence.** A positive attitude is a great way to combat test anxiety. This is no time to be humble or shy. Stand in front of the mirror and say to your reflection, "I'm prepared. I'm full of self-confidence. I'm going to ace this test. I know I can do it." Say it into a tape recorder and play it back once a day. If you hear it often enough, you will believe it.
- ▶ **Fight negative messages.** Every time someone starts telling you how hard the exam is or how it is almost impossible to get a high score, start telling them your self-confidence messages above. If the someone with the negative messages is you, telling yourself that you don't do well on exams or you just cannot do this, don't listen. Turn on your tape recorder and listen to your self-confidence messages.
- ▶ **Visualize.** Imagine yourself reporting for your first day on the job. Picture the clothes you will wear, the interior of your new office, and you greeting your new colleagues. Visualizing success can help make it happen—and it reminds you why you are preparing for the exam so diligently.
- ▶ **Exercise.** Physical activity helps calm your body and focus your mind. Besides, being in good physical shape can actually help you do well on the exam. Go for a run, lift weights, go swimming—and do it regularly.

Stress Management on Test Day

There are several ways you can bring down your level of test anxiety on test day. To find a comfort level, practice these strategies in the weeks before the test, and use the ones that work best for you.

- ▶ **Deep breathing.** Take a deep breath while you count to five. Hold it for a count of one, then let it out on a count of five. Repeat several times.
- ▶ **Move your body.** Try rolling your head in a circle. Rotate your shoulders. Shake your hands from the wrist. Many people find these movements very relaxing.
- ▶ **Visualize again.** Think of the place where you are most relaxed: lying on the beach in the sun, walking through the park, or wherever. Now close your eyes and imagine you are

actually there. If you practice in advance, you will find that you need only a few seconds of this exercise to increase your sense of well-being.

When anxiety threatens to overwhelm you right there during the exam, there are still things you can do to manage your stress level:

► **Repeat your self-confidence messages.** You should have them memorized by now. Say them silently to yourself, and believe them.
► **Visualize one more time.** This time, visualize yourself moving smoothly and quickly through the test, answering every question correctly and finishing just before time is up. Like most visualization techniques, this one works best if you have practiced it ahead of time.
► **Find an easy question.** Skim over the test until you find an easy question, and answer it. Getting even one circle filled in gets you into the test-taking groove.
► **Take a mental break.** Everyone loses concentration once in a while during a long test. It is normal, so you shouldn't worry about it. Instead, accept what has happened. Say to yourself, "Hey, I lost it there for a minute. My brain is taking a break." Put down your pencil, close your eyes, and do some deep breathing for a few seconds. Then you are ready to go back to work.

Try these techniques ahead of time, and see how well they work for you.

TEST STRESS TEST

You need to worry about test anxiety only if it is extreme enough to impair your performance. The following questionnaire will provide a diagnosis of your level of test anxiety. In the blank before each statement, write the number that most accurately describes your experience.

0 = Never   1 = Once or twice   2 = Sometimes   3 = Often

_____ I have gotten so nervous before an exam that I simply put down the books and didn't study for it.

_____ I have experienced disabling physical symptoms such as vomiting and severe headaches because I was nervous about an exam.

_____ I have simply not showed up for an exam because I was scared to take it.

_____ I have experienced dizziness and disorientation while taking an exam.

_____ I have had trouble filling in the little circles because my hands were shaking too hard.

_____ I have failed an exam because I was too nervous to complete it.

_____ **Total:** Add up the numbers in the blanks above.

Your Test Stress Score

Here are the steps you should take, depending on your score. If you scored:

- 0–2: your level of test anxiety is nothing to worry about; it is probably just enough to give you the motivation to excel.
- 3–6: your test anxiety may be enough to impair your performance, and you should practice the stress management techniques listed in this section to try to bring your test anxiety down to manageable levels.
- 7+: your level of test anxiety is a serious concern. In addition to practicing the stress management techniques listed in this section, you may want to seek additional professional help. Call your local high school or community college and ask for the academic counselor. Tell the counselor that you have a level of test anxiety that sometimes keeps you from being able to take an exam. The counselor may be willing to help you or may suggest someone else you should talk to.

▶ STEP 3: MAKE A PLAN

Time to complete: 50 minutes
Activity: Construct a study plan

Maybe the most important thing you can do to get control of yourself and your exam is to make a study plan. Too many people fail to prepare simply because they fail to plan. Spending hours on the day before the exam poring over sample test questions not only raises your level of test anxiety, it also is simply no substitute for careful preparation and practice.

Don't fall into the cram trap. Take control of your preparation time by mapping out a study schedule. If you are the kind of person who needs deadlines and assignments to motivate you for a project, here they are. If you are the kind of person who doesn't like to follow other people's plans, you can use the suggested schedules here to construct your own.

Even more important than making a plan is making a commitment. You cannot review everything you need to know for a Civil Service test in one night. You have to set aside some time every day for study and practice. Try for at least 20 minutes a day. Twenty minutes daily will do you much more good than one two-hour session each week.

If you have months before the exam, you are very lucky. But don't let that long time span keep you from studying. Start now. Even ten minutes a day, with half an hour or more on weekends, can make a big difference in your score—and in your chances of getting the job you want.

Schedule A: The 30-Day Plan

If you have at least a month before you take your test, you have plenty of time to prepare— as long as you don't waste it! If you have less than a month, turn to Schedule B.

TIME	PREPARATION
Day 1–2	Read the Introduction of this book. Also, skim over the written materials from any courses or training programs you may have taken, particularly noting areas you expect to be emphasized on the exam and areas you don't remember well.
Day 3	Read Chapter 3, Vocabulary in Context, and practice these basic skills by answering Questions 1–15. Score yourself by referring to the answer explanations at the end of the chapter.
Day 4	Continue Chapter 3 by answering Questions 16–30. Score yourself by referring to the answer explanations at the end of the chapter.
Day 5	Review any concepts in Chapter 3 that you feel are necessary for you to reevaluate. Answer Questions 31–40 and score yourself. Check your answers at the end of the chapter.
Day 6	Answer Questions 41–50 in Chapter 3. Score yourself and make sure that you understand all of the concepts covered in this chapter.
Day 7	Read Chapter 4, Synonyms and Antonyms, and answer Questions 1-12. Score yourself.
Day 8	Review any Chapter 4 concepts that you feel you may need more time to absorb. Answer Questions 13–25 and score yourself.
Day 9	Answer Questions 26–50 in Chapter 4. Score yourself and make sure that you understand all of the concepts covered in this chapter.
Day 10	Read Chapter 5, Reading Comprehension, and answer Questions 1–10 and score yourself.
Day 11	Review any Chapter 5 concepts that you feel you may need more time to absorb. Answer Questions 11–30 and score yourself.
Day 12	Answer Questions 31–50 in Chapter 5. Score yourself and make sure that you understand all of the concepts covered in this chapter.
Day 13	Read Chapter 6, Grammar, answer Questions 1–10, and score yourself.
Day 14	Review any Chapter 6 concepts that you feel you may need more time to absorb. Answer Questions 11–30 and score yourself.
Day 15	Work through Questions 31–50 in Chapter 6. Score yourself and make sure that you understand all of the concepts covered in this chapter.
Day 16	Read Chapter 7, Spelling, answer Questions 1–10, and score yourself.
Day 17	Review any Chapter 7 concepts that you feel you may need more time to absorb. Answer Questions 11–30 and score yourself.

Day 18	Work through Questions 31–50 in Chapter 7. Score yourself and make sure that you understand all of the concepts covered in this chapter.
Day 19	Begin to review the Commonly Tested Words in Chapter 2. Highlight any words that you think may give you difficulty.
Day 20	Turn to the Prefixes, Suffixes, and Word Roots on page 56. Review the Prefixes and Suffixes and highlight any that you think are hard for you to remember.
Day 21	Complete your review of the Commonly Tested Words and highlight unfamiliar words.
Day 22	Review the Word Roots and highlight any that you think are hard for you to remember.
Day 23	Compare your knowledge of Prefixes, Suffixes, and Word Roots to the Commonly Tested Words to see if you notice the ways these word elements are used in words.
Day 24	Return to your highlighted words and review them. Choose ten words and quiz yourself to see if you can remember the definitions. See if you can use those words in sentences.
Day 25	In Chapter 8, take Practice Test 1. Score yourself and review any incorrect questions.
Day 26	Review any concepts that you feel are necessary for you to re-evaluate. Work through similar questions in the appropriate chapters.
Day 27	In Chapter 9, take Practice Test 2. Score yourself and review any incorrect questions.
Day 28	Review any concepts that you feel you may need more time to absorb. Work through similar questions in the appropriate chapters.
Day 29	Identify your weaknesses in the Practice Tests and review the coordinating chapters to review those skills. Choose ten more words from your highlighted vocabulary list and quiz yourself to see if you can remember the definitions. See if you can use those words in sentences.
Day before the exam	Relax. Do something unrelated to the exam and go to bed at a reasonable hour.

Schedule B: The 14-Day Plan

If you have two weeks or less before you take your exam, you have your work cut out for you. Use this 14-day schedule to help you make the most of your time.

TIME	PREPARATION
Day 1	Read the Introduction and Chapter 1.
Day 2	Complete Chapter 3, Vocabulary in Context—including the Practice Questions. Review any incorrect answers.
Day 3	Complete Chapter 4, Synonyms and Antonyms—including the Practice Questions. Review any incorrect answers.
Day 4	Complete Chapter 5, Reading Comprehension—including the Practice Questions. Review any incorrect answers.
Day 5	Complete Chapter 6, Grammar—including the Practice Questions. Review any incorrect answers.
Day 6	Complete Chapter 7, Spelling—including the Practice Questions. Review any incorrect answers.
Day 7	Review the Commonly Tested Words in Chapter 2 and highlight all unfamiliar words.
Day 8	Review the Prefixes, Suffixes, and Word Roots list and highlight any troublesome areas.
Day 9	Review the words you highlighted in the Commonly Tested Words.
Day 10	Complete Chapter 8, Practice Test 1, and score yourself. Review all of the questions that you missed.
Day 11	Review any concepts that you feel are necessary for you to reassess. Work through similar questions in appropriate chapters.
Day 12	Complete Chapter 9, Practice Test 2, and score yourself. Review all of the questions that you missed.
Day 13	Review any concepts that you feel are necessary for you to reassess. Work through similar questions in appropriate chapters. Make sure you understand them before you finish.
Day before the exam	Relax. Do something unrelated to the exam and go to bed at a reasonable hour.

▶ STEP 4: LEARN TO MANAGE YOUR TIME

Time to complete: 10 minutes to read, many hours of practice!
Activities: Practice these strategies as you take the sample tests in this book

Steps 4, 5, and 6 of the LearningExpress Test Preparation System put you in charge of your exam by showing you test-taking strategies that work. Practice these strategies as you take the sample tests in this book, and then you can use them on test day.

First, take control of your time on the exam. Civil Service exams have a time limit, which may give you more than enough time to complete all the questions—or may not. It is a terrible feeling to hear the examiner say, "Five minutes left," when you are only three-quarters of the way through the test. Here are some tips to keep that from happening to *you*.

- ▶ **Follow directions**. If the directions are given orally, listen closely. If they are written on the exam booklet, read them carefully. Ask questions *before* the exam begins if there is anything you don't understand. If you are allowed to write in your exam booklet, write down the beginning time and the ending time of the exam.
- ▶ **Pace yourself**. Glance at your watch every few minutes and compare the time to the amount you have completed on the test. When one quarter of the time has elapsed, you should be a quarter of the way through the section, and so on. If you are falling behind, pick up the pace a bit.
- ▶ **Keep moving**. Do not waste time on one question. If you don't know the answer, skip the question and move on. Circle the number of the question in your test booklet in case you have time to come back to it later.
- ▶ **Keep track of your place on the answer sheet**. If you skip a question, make sure you skip it on the answer sheet too. Check yourself every 5–10 questions to make sure the question number and the answer sheet number are still the same.
- ▶ **Don't rush**. Though you should keep moving, rushing will not help. Try to keep calm and work methodically and quickly.

▶ STEP 5: LEARN TO USE THE PROCESS OF ELIMINATION

Time to complete: 20 minutes
Activity: Complete worksheet on Using the Process of Elimination

After time management, your next most important tool for taking control of your exam is using the process of elimination wisely. It is standard test-taking wisdom that you should always read all the answer choices before choosing your answer. This helps you find the right answer by eliminating wrong answer choices.

Choosing the Right Answer by Process of Elimination

As you read a question, you may find it helpful to underline important information or take notes about what you are reading. When you get to the heart of the question, circle it and make sure you understand what it is asking. If you are not sure of what is being asked, you will never know whether you have chosen the right answer. What you do next depends on the type of question you are answering.

▶ If it is a vocabulary question, take a quick look at the answer choices for some clues. Sometimes this helps to put the question in a new perspective and makes it easier to answer. Then make a plan of attack to determine the answer. This book will help you come up with strategies to answer difficult questions.

▶ Otherwise, follow this simple process of elimination plan to manage your testing time as efficiently as possible: Read each answer choice and make a quick decision about what to do with it, marking your test book accordingly:
  ■ The answer seems reasonable; keep it. Put a smiley face next to the answer.
  ■ The answer is awful. Get rid of it. Put an X next to the answer.
  ■ You can't make up your mind about the answer, or you do not understand it. Keep it for now. Put a **?** next to it.

Whatever you do, do not waste time with any one answer choice. If you can't figure out what an answer choice means, don't worry about it. If it is the right answer, you will probably be able to eliminate all the others, and if it is the wrong answer, another answer will stand out as the obvious right answer.

If you have not eliminated any answers at all, skip the question temporarily, but don't forget to mark the question so you can come back to it later if you have time. If the test has no penalty for wrong answers, and you are certain that you could never answer this question in a million years, pick an answer and move on.

If you have eliminated all but one answer, just reread the circled part of the question to make sure you are answering exactly what is asked. Mark your answer sheet and move on to the next question.

If you have eliminated some, but not all, of the answer choices, compare the remaining answers as you look for similarities and differences, reasoning your way through these choices. Try to eliminate those choices that do not seem as strong to you. But *do not* eliminate an answer just because you don't understand it. If you have narrowed it down to a single answer, check it against the circled question to be sure you have answered it. Then mark your answer sheet and move on. If you are down to only two or three answer choices, you have improved your odds of getting the question right. Make an educated guess and move on. However, if you think you can do better with more time, mark the question as one to return to later.

If You Are Penalized for Wrong Answers

You must know whether you will be penalized for wrong answers before you begin the test. If you do not know, ask the proctor before the test begins. Whether you make a guess or not depends upon the penalty. Some standardized tests are scored in such a way that every wrong answer reduces your score by a fraction of a point, and these can really add up against you! Whatever the penalty, if you can eliminate enough choices to make the odds of answering the question better than the penalty for getting it wrong, make a guess. This is called educated guessing.

Let's imagine you are taking a test in which each answer has five choices and you are penalized $\frac{1}{4}$ of a point for each wrong answer. If you cannot eliminate any of the answer choices, you are better off leaving the answer blank, because the odds of guessing correctly are one in five. However, if you can eliminate two of the choices as definitely wrong, the odds are now in your favor. You have a one in three chance of answering the question correctly. Fortunately, few tests are scored using such elaborate means, but if your test is one of them, know the penalties and calculate your odds before you take a guess on a question.

If You Finish Early

If you finish before the time is up for any section of the exam, use the time you have left to do the following:

- ▶ Go back to questions you could not answer and try them again.
- ▶ Check your work on all the other questions. If you have a good reason for thinking a response is wrong, change it.
- ▶ Review your answer sheet. Make sure that you have put the answers in the right places and that you have marked only one answer for each question. (Most tests are scored in such a way that questions with more than one answer are marked wrong.)
- ▶ If you have erased an answer, make sure you have done a good job of it.
- ▶ Check for stray marks on your answer sheet that could distort your score.

Whatever you do, do not waste time when you have finished a test section. Make every second count by checking your work over and over again until time is called.

Now try using your powers of elimination as you complete the exercise called "Using the Process of Elimination." The answer explanations that follow show one possible way you might use this process to arrive at the right answer.

The process of elimination—knowing when to guess—is your tool for the next step.

USING THE PROCESS OF ELIMINATION

Use the process of elimination to answer the following questions.

1. ⓐ ⓑ ⓒ ⓓ
2. ⓐ ⓑ ⓒ ⓓ
3. ⓐ ⓑ ⓒ ⓓ
4. ⓐ ⓑ ⓒ ⓓ

1. Ilsa is as old as Meghan will be in five years. The difference between Ed's age and Meghan's age is twice the difference between Ilsa's age and Meghan's age. Ed is 29. How old is Ilsa?
   a. 4
   b. 10
   c. 19
   d. 24

2. "All drivers of commercial vehicles must carry a valid commercial driver's license whenever operating a commercial vehicle." According to this sentence, which of the following people need NOT carry a commercial driver's license?
   a. a truck driver idling his engine while waiting to be directed to a loading dock
   b. a bus operator backing her bus out of the way of another bus in the bus lot
   c. a taxi driver driving his personal car to the grocery store
   d. a limousine driver taking the limousine to her home after dropping off her last passenger of the evening

3. Smoking tobacco has been linked to
   a. an increased risk of stroke and heart attack.
   b. all forms of respiratory disease.
   c. increasing mortality rates over the past ten years.
   d. juvenile delinquency.

4. Which of the following words is spelled correctly?
   a. incorrigible
   b. outragous
   c. domestickated
   d. understandible

Answers

Here are the answers, as well as some suggestions as to how you might have used the process of elimination to find them.

1. **d.** You should have eliminated choice **a** immediately. Ilsa can't be four years old if Meghan is going to be Ilsa's age in five years. The best way to eliminate other answer choices is to try plugging them in to the information given in the problem. For instance, for choice **b**, if Ilsa is 10, then Meghan must be 5. The difference in their ages is 5. The difference between Ed's age, 29, and Meghan's age, 5, is 24. Is 24 equal to 2 times 5? No. Then choice **b** is wrong. You could eliminate choice **c** in the same way and be left with choice **d**.

2. **c**. Note the word *not* in the question, and go through the answers one by one. Is the truck driver in choice **a** "operating a commercial vehicle"? Yes, idling counts as "operating," so he needs to have a commercial driver's license. Likewise, the bus operator in choice **b** is operating a commercial vehicle; the question doesn't say the operator has to be on the street. The

limo driver in choice **d** is operating a commercial vehicle, even if it doesn't have a passenger in it. However, the cabbie in choice **c** is not operating a commercial vehicle, but his own private car.

3. **a.** You could eliminate choice **b** simply because of the presence of the word *all*. Such absolutes hardly ever appear in correct answer choices. Choice **c** looks attractive until you think a little about what you know—aren't fewer people smoking these days, rather than more? So, how could smoking be responsible for a higher mortality rate? (If you didn't know that "mortality rate" means the rate at which people die, you might keep this choice as a possibility, but you would still be able to eliminate two answers and have only two to choose from.) Choice **d** can't be proven, so you could eliminate that one, too. Now you are left with the correct choice, **a.**

4. **a.** How you used the process of elimination here depends on which words you recognized as being spelled incorrectly. If you knew that the correct spellings were *outrageous, domesticated,* and *understandable,* then you were home free.

▶ STEP 6: KNOW WHEN TO GUESS

Time to complete: 20 minutes
Activity: Complete worksheet on Your Guessing Ability

Armed with the process of elimination, you are ready to take control of one of the big questions in test-taking: Should I guess? The first and main answer is *yes.* Some exams have a guessing penalty; check with the administrators of your particular exam to see if this is the case. In many instances, the number of questions you answer correctly yields your raw score. So you have nothing to lose and everything to gain by guessing if you know how to make an educated guess.

The more complicated answer to the question, "Should I guess?" depends on you, your personality, and your "guessing intuition." There are two things you need to know about yourself before you go into the exam:

▶ Are you a risk-taker?
▶ Are you a good guesser?

You will have to decide about your risk-taking quotient on your own. To find out if you are a good guesser, complete the following worksheet called *Your Guessing Ability.* Even if you are a play-it-safe person with terrible intuition, guessing is sometimes a good strategy. The best thing would be if you could overcome your anxieties and go ahead and mark an answer. But you may want to have a sense of how good your intuition is before you go into the exam.

YOUR GUESSING ABILITY

The following are ten really hard questions. You are not supposed to know the answers. Rather, this is an assessment of your ability to guess when you do not have a clue. Read each question carefully, just as if you did expect to answer it. If you have any knowledge at all of the subject of the question, use that knowledge to help you eliminate wrong answer choices. Use this answer grid to fill in your answers to the questions.

1.	ⓐ	ⓑ	ⓒ	ⓓ	**6.**	ⓐ	ⓑ	ⓒ	ⓓ
2.	ⓐ	ⓑ	ⓒ	ⓓ	**7.**	ⓐ	ⓑ	ⓒ	ⓓ
3.	ⓐ	ⓑ	ⓒ	ⓓ	**8.**	ⓐ	ⓑ	ⓒ	ⓓ
4.	ⓐ	ⓑ	ⓒ	ⓓ	**9.**	ⓐ	ⓑ	ⓒ	ⓓ
5.	ⓐ	ⓑ	ⓒ	ⓓ	**10.**	ⓐ	ⓑ	ⓒ	ⓓ

1. September 7 is Independence Day in
   a. India.
   b. Costa Rica.
   c. Brazil.
   d. Australia.

2. Which of the following is the formula for determining the momentum of an object?
   a. $p = mv$
   b. $F = ma$
   c. $P = IV$
   d. $E = mc^2$

3. Because of the expansion of the universe, the stars and other celestial bodies are all moving away from each other. This phenomenon is known as
   a. Newton's first law.
   b. the big bang.
   c. gravitational collapse.
   d. Hubble flow.

4. American author Gertrude Stein was born in
   a. 1713.
   b. 1830.
   c. 1874.
   d. 1901.

5. Which of the following is NOT one of the Five Classics attributed to Confucius?
   a. the I Ching
   b. the Book of Holiness
   c. the Spring and Autumn Annals
   d. the Book of History

6. The religious and philosophical doctrine stating that the universe is constantly in a struggle between good and evil is known as
   a. Pelagianism.
   b. Manichaeanism.
   c. neo-Hegelianism.
   d. Epicureanism.

7. The third Chief Justice of the U.S. Supreme Court was
   a. John Blair.
   b. William Cushing.
   c. James Wilson.
   d. John Jay.

8. Which of the following is the poisonous portion of a daffodil?
   a. the bulb
   b. the leaves
   c. the stem
   d. the flowers

9. The winner of the Masters golf tournament in 1953 was
   a. Sam Snead.
   b. Cary Middlecoff.
   c. Arnold Palmer.
   d. Ben Hogan.

10. The state with the highest per capita personal income in 1980 was
    a. Alaska.
    b. Connecticut.
    c. New York.
    d. Texas.

Answers

Check your answers against the correct answers below.

1. c.
2. a.
3. d.
4. c.
5. b.
6. b.
7. b.
8. a.
9. d.
10. a.

How Did You Do?

You may have simply been lucky and actually known the answers to one or two questions. In addition, your guessing was more successful if you were able to use the process of elimination on any of the questions. Maybe you did not know who the third Chief Justice was (question 7), but you knew that John Jay was the first. In that case, you would have eliminated choice **d** and therefore improved your odds of guessing right from one in four to one in three.

According to probability, you should get $2\frac{1}{2}$ answers correct, so getting either two or three right would be average. If you got four or more right, you may be a really terrific guesser. If you got one or none right, you may want to decide not to guess.

Keep in mind, though, that this is only a small sample. You should continue to keep track of your guessing ability as you work through the sample questions in this book. Circle the numbers of questions you guess; or, if you do not have time during the practice tests, go back afterward and try to remember which questions you guessed. Remember, on a test with four answer choices, your chances of getting a right answer is one in four. So keep a separate "guessing" score for each exam. On how many questions did you guess? How many of those did you get right? If the number you got right is at least one-fourth of the number of questions you guessed, you are at least an average guesser, maybe better—and you should always go ahead and guess on the real exam. If the number you got right is significantly lower than one-fourth of the number you guessed, you should not guess on exams where there is a guessing penalty—unless you can eliminate a wrong answer. If there is no guessing penalty, you would be safe in guessing. You may feel more comfortable, though, if you guess only selectively—when you can eliminate a wrong answer or at least when you have a good feeling about one of the answer choices.

▶ STEP 7: REACH YOUR PEAK PERFORMANCE ZONE

Time to complete: 10 minutes to read; weeks to complete
Activity: Complete the Physical Preparation Checklist

To get ready for the challenge of a big exam, you have to take control of your physical as well as your mental state. Exercise, proper diet, and rest will ensure that your body works with, rather than against, your mind on test day, as well as during your preparation time.

Exercise

If you do not already have a regular exercise program going, the time during which you are preparing for an exam is actually an excellent time to start one. If you are already keeping fit—or trying to get that way—don't let the pressure of preparing for an exam fool you into quitting now. Exercise helps reduce stress by pumping wonderful good-feeling hormones called endorphins into your system. It also increases the oxygen supply throughout your body and your brain, so you will be at peak performance on test day.

A half hour of vigorous activity—enough to raise a sweat—every day should be your aim. If you are really pressed for time, every other day is okay. Choose an activity you like and get out there and do it. Jogging with a friend, for example, might make the time go faster; so might listening to music.

But remember, do not overdo it. You don't want to exhaust yourself. Moderation is the key.

Diet

In order to succeed mentally, it's important to give your body the fuel it needs to stay healthy. First of all, cut out the junk. Go easy on caffeine and nicotine, and eliminate any alcohol for at least two weeks before the exam.

What your body needs for peak performance is simply a balanced diet. Eat plenty of fruits and vegetables, along with protein and carbohydrates. Foods that are high in lecithin (an amino acid), such as fish and beans, are especially good "brain foods."

Rest

You probably know how much sleep you need every night to be at your best, even if you do not always get it. Make sure you do get that much sleep, though, for at least a week before the exam. Moderation is important here, too. Extra sleep will just make you groggy.

If you are not a morning person and your exam will be given in the morning, you should reset your internal clock so that your body does not think you are taking an exam at 3 A.M. You have to start this process well before the exam. The way it works is to get up half an hour earlier each morning, and then go to bed half an hour earlier that night. Do not try it the other way around; you will just toss and turn if you go to bed early without getting up early. The next morning, get up another half hour earlier, and so on. How long you will have to do this depends on how late you are used to getting up. Use the *Physical Preparation Checklist* on the next page to make sure you are in tip-top form.

▶ STEP 8: GET YOUR ACT TOGETHER

Time to complete: 10 minutes to read; time to complete will vary
Activity: Complete Final Preparations worksheet

When you feel healthy and confident, you are ready to take charge of test anxiety, test preparation, and test-taking strategies. Now it is time to make charts and gather the materials you need to take to the exam.

Gather Your Materials

The night before the exam, lay out the clothes you will wear and the materials you have to bring with you to the exam. Plan on dressing in layers, because you will not have any control over the temperature of the exam room. Have a sweater or jacket you can take off if it is warm. Use the checklist on the worksheet entitled *Final Preparations* on page 21 to help you pull together what you will need.

Don't Skip Breakfast

Even if you do not usually eat breakfast, do so on exam morning. A cup of coffee does not count. Do not eat doughnuts or other sweet foods, either. A sugar high will leave you with a sugar low in the middle of the exam. A mix of protein and carbohydrates is best: cereal with milk, or eggs with toast, will do your body a world of good.

PHYSICAL PREPARATION CHECKLIST

For the week before the test, write down what physical exercise you engaged in and for how long. Then write down what you ate for each meal. Remember, you are trying for at least half an hour of exercise every other day (preferably every day) and a balanced diet that's light on junk food.

Exam minus 7 days

Exercise: _____ for _____ minutes

Breakfast: _____

Lunch: _____

Dinner: _____

Snacks: _____

Exam minus 6 days

Exercise: _____ for minutes

Breakfast: _____

Lunch: _____

Dinner: _____

Snacks: _____

Exam minus 5 days

Exercise: _____ for _____ minutes

Breakfast: _____

Lunch: _____

Dinner: _____

Snacks: _____

Exam minus 4 days

Exercise: _____ for _____ minutes

Breakfast: _____

Lunch: _____

Dinner: _____

Snacks: _____

Exam minus 3 days

Exercise: _____ for _____ minutes

Breakfast: _____

Lunch: _____

Dinner: _____

Snacks: _____

Exam minus 2 days

Exercise: _____ for _____ minutes

Breakfast: _____

Lunch: _____

Dinner: _____

Snacks: _____

Exam minus 1 day

Exercise: _____ for _____ minutes

Breakfast: _____

Lunch: _____

Dinner: _____

Snacks: _____

▶ STEP 9: DO IT!

Time to complete: 10 minutes, plus test-taking time
Activity: Ace Your Test

Fast forward to exam day. You are ready. You made a study plan and followed through. You practiced your test-taking strategies while working through this book. You are in control of your physical, mental, and emotional state. You know when and where to show up and what to bring with you. In other words, you are better prepared than most of the other people taking the test with you.

Just one more thing. When you complete the exam, you will have earned a reward. Plan a celebration. Call your friends and get together for a party, or have a nice dinner for two—whatever your heart desires. Give yourself something to look forward to.

And then do it. Go into the exam, full of confidence, armed with the test-taking strategies you have practiced until they are second nature. You are in control of yourself, your environment, and your performance on exam day. You are ready to succeed. So do it. Go in there and ace the exam. And then look forward to your new career.

FINAL PREPARATIONS

Getting to the Exam Site

Location of exam: _____

Date of exam: _____

Time of exam: _____

Do I know how to get to the exam site? Yes _____ No _____

If no, make a trial run.

Time it will take to get to the exam site: _____

Things to Lay Out the Night Before

Clothes I will wear _____

Sweater/jacket _____

Watch _____

Photo ID _____

Admission card _____

Four No. 2 pencils _____

_____

_____

Resources—
Commonly Tested
Words, Prefixes,
Suffixes, and
Word Roots for
Successful Studying

Before embarking on any vocabulary study, it is a good idea to build your bank of words. The greater your base of word knowledge, the easier it will be for you to answer any vocabulary question that comes your way. Rather than having you read the dictionary, this chapter narrows down your study list by giving you 500 words that are commonly found on vocabulary tests. Each night, target ten words that you feel you do not know. Read the definitions and the way each word is used in a sentence. Try to use the words in conversation, in your reports or memos, or even in an e-mail. The more you use a word, the more familiar it will become to you. When words are familiar, you can count on them to help you with all forms of communication—or to pass any kind of test.

▶ COMMONLY TESTED VOCABULARY WORDS

aberration (ăb·ĕ·′ray·shŏn) *n.* deviation from what is normal, distortion. *His new scientific theory was deemed an aberration by his very conservative colleagues.*

abeyance (ă·′bay·ăns) *n.* suspension, being temporarily suspended or set aside. *Construction of the highway is in abeyance until we get agency approval.*

abhor (ab·′hohr) *v.* to regard with horror, detest. *I abhor such hypocrisy.*

abjure (ab·′joor) *v.* 1. to repudiate, renounce under oath 2. to give up or reject. *When Joseph became a citizen, he had to abjure his allegiance to his country of origin.*

abrogate ('ab·rŏ·gayt) *v.* to abolish, do away with, or annul by authority. *It was unclear if the judge would abrogate the lower court's ruling.*

abscond (ab·'skond) *v.* to run away secretly and hide, often in order to avoid arrest or prosecution. *Criminals will often head south and abscond with stolen goods to Mexico.*

absolution (ab·sŏ·'loo·shŏn) *n.* 1. an absolving or clearing from blame or guilt 2. a formal declaration of forgiveness, redemption. *The jury granted Alan the absolution he deserved.*

abstain (ab·'stayn) *v.* to choose to refrain from something, especially to refrain from voting. *I have decided to abstain on this issue.*

abstruse (ab·'stroos) *adj.* difficult to comprehend, obscure. *Albert Einstein's abstruse calculations can be understood by only a few people.*

abysmal (ă·'biz·măl) *adj.* 1. extreme, very profound, limitless 2. extremely bad. *Tom's last-place finish in the race was an abysmal turn of events for the team.*

accolade ('ak·ŏ·layd) *n.* 1. praise or approval 2. a ceremonial embrace in greeting 3. a ceremonious tap on the shoulder with a sword to mark the conferring of knighthood. *He received accolades from his superiors for finding ways to cut costs and increase productivity.*

accretion (ă·'kree·shŏn) *n.* 1. growth or increase by gradual, successive addition; building up 2. (in biology) the growing together of parts that are normally separate. *The accretion of sediment in the harbor channel caused boats to run aground.*

acrid ('ak·rid) *adj.* 1. having an unpleasantly bitter, sharp taste or smell 2. bitter or caustic in language or manner. *The burning tires in the junkyard gave off an acrid odor.*

ad hoc (ad 'hok) *adj.* for a specific, often temporary, purpose; for this case only. *She acted as the ad hoc scout leader while Mr. Davis—the official leader—was ill.*

adamant ('ad·ă·mănt) *adj.* 1. unyielding to requests, appeals, or reason 2. firm, inflexible. *The senator was adamant that no changes would be made to the defense budget.*

addle ('ad·ĕl) *v.* 1. to muddle or confuse 2. to become rotten, as in an egg. *The jury found the defendant addled at the end of the prosecuting attorney's questions.*

ado (ă·'doo) *n.* fuss, trouble, bother. *Without much ado, she completed her book report.*

aficionado (ă·fish·yŏ·'nah·doh) *n.* a fan or devotee, especially of a sport or pastime. *The Jeffersons' attendance at every game proved that they were true aficionados of baseball.*

alacrity (ă·'lak·ri·tee) *n.* a cheerful willingness; being happily ready and eager. *The alacrity she brought to her job helped her move up the corporate ladder quickly.*

allay (ă·'lay) *v.* 1. to reduce the intensity of, alleviate 2. to calm, put to rest. *The remarks by the CEO did not allay the concerns of the employees.*

altercation (awl·tĕr·ˈkay·shŏn) *n.* a heated dispute or quarrel. *To prevent an altercation at social functions, one should avoid discussing politics and religion.*

ambivalent (am·ˈbiv·ă·lĕnt) *adj.* having mixed or conflicting feelings about a person, thing, or situation; uncertain. *She was ambivalent about the proposal for the shopping center because she understood the arguments both for and against its construction.*

ameliorate (ă·ˈmeel·yŏ·rayt) *v.* to make or become better, to improve. *The diplomat was able to ameliorate the tense situation between the two nations.*

amorphous (ă·ˈmor·fŭs) *adj.* having no definite shape or form; shapeless. *The amorphous cloud of steam drifted over her head.*

amulet (ˈam·yŭ·lit) *n.* something worn around the neck as a charm against evil. *The princess wore an amulet after being cursed by a wizard.*

anachronism (ă·ˈnak·rŏ·niz·ĕm) *n.* 1. something that is placed into an incorrect historical period 2. a person, custom, or idea that is out of date. *The authenticity and credibility of the 1920s movie was damaged by the many anachronisms that appeared throughout the scenes.*

anarchy (ˈan·ăr·kee) *n.* 1. the complete absence of government or control, resulting in lawlessness 2. political disorder and confusion. *The days immediately following the revolution were marked by anarchy.*

anomaly (ă·ˈnom·ă·lee) *n.* something that deviates from the general rule or usual form; one that is irregular, peculiar or abnormal. *Winning millions of dollars from a slot machine would be considered an anomaly.*

antipathy (an·ˈtip·ă·thee) *n.* 1. a strong aversion or dislike 2. an object of aversion. *It is a moment I recall with great antipathy.*

antithesis (an·ˈtith·ĕ·sis) *n.* the direct or exact opposite, opposition or contrast. *Martin's parenting style is the antithesis of mine.*

apathetic (ap·ă·ˈthet·ik) *adj.* feeling or showing a lack of interest, concern, or emotion; indifferent, unresponsive. *Ms. Brownstone was distressed by how apathetic her eighth grade students were.*

aperture (ˈap·ĕr·chŭr) *n.* an opening or gap, especially one that lets in light. *The aperture setting on a camera has to be set perfectly to ensure that pictures will have enough light.*

apex (ˈay·peks) *n.* 1. the highest point 2. tip, pointed end. *Upon reaching the apex of the mountain, the climbers placed their flag in the snow.*

apocalypse (ă·ˈpok·ă·lips) *n.* a cataclysmic event bringing about total devastation or the end of the world. *Many people feared an apocalypse would immediately follow the development of nuclear weapons.*

apostate (ă·ˈpos·tayt) *n.* one who abandons long-held religious or political convictions. *Disillusioned with the religious life, Reverend Gift lost his faith and left the ministry, not caring if he'd be seen as an apostate by colleagues who chose to remain.*

apotheosis (ă·poth·i·ˈoh·sis) *n.* deification, an exalted or glorified ideal. *Lancelot was the apotheosis of chivalry until he met Guinevere.*

appease (ă·ˈpeez) *v.* to make calm or quiet, soothe; to still or pacify. *His ability to appease his constituents helped him win reelection.*

apprise (ă·ˈprīz) *v.* to inform, give notice to. *Part of Susan's job as a public defender was to apprise people of their legal rights.*

approbation (ap·rŏ·ˈbay·shŏn) *n.* approval. *The local authorities issued an approbation to close the street for a festival on St. Patrick's Day.*

appropriate (ă·ˈproh·pree·ayt) *v.* to take for one's own use, often without permission; to set aside for a special purpose. *The state legislature will appropriate two million dollars from the annual budget to build a new bridge on the interstate highway.*

apropos (ap·rŏ·ˈpoh) *adj.* appropriate to the situation; suitable to what is being said or done. *The chairman's remarks about the founding fathers were apropos since it was the fourth of July.*

arcane (ahr·ˈkayn) *adj.* mysterious, secret, beyond comprehension. *A number of college students in the 1980s became involved in the arcane game known as "Dungeons and Dragons."*

archaic (ahr·ˈkay·ik) *adj.* belonging to former or ancient times; characteristic of the past. *Samantha laughed at her grandfather's archaic views of dating and relationships.*

archetype (ˈahr·ki·tīp) *n.* an original model from which others are copied; original pattern or prototype. *Elvis Presley served as the archetype for rock and roll performers in the 1950s.*

ardor (ˈahr·dŏr) *n.* fiery intensity of feeling; passionate enthusiasm, zeal. *The ardor Larry brought to the campaign made him a natural campaign spokesperson.*

arduous (ˈahr·joo·ŭs) *adj.* 1. very difficult, laborious; requiring great effort 2. difficult to traverse or surmount. *Commander Shackleton's arduous journey through the Arctic has become the subject of many books and movies.*

ascetic (ă·ˈset·ik) *adj.* practicing self-denial, not allowing oneself pleasures or luxuries; austere. *Some religions require their leaders to lead an ascetic lifestyle as an example to their followers.*

askew (ă·ˈskyoo) *adj. & adv.* crooked, not straight or level; to one side. *Even the pictures on the wall stood askew after my five-year-old son's birthday party.*

asperity (ă·ˈsper·i·tee) *n.* harshness, severity; roughness of manner, ill temper, irritability. *The asperity that Marvin, the grumpy accountant, brought to the meetings usually resulted in an early adjournment.*

assay (ă·ˈsay) *v.* 1. to try, put to a test 2. to examine 3. to judge critically, evaluate after an analysis. *The chief engineer wanted a laboratory to assay the steel before using it in the construction project.*

assiduous (ă·ˈsij·oo·ŭs) *adj.* diligent, persevering, unremitting; constant in application or attention. *The nurses in the intensive care unit are known for providing assiduous care to their patients.*

assuage (ă·ˈswayj) *v.* to make something less severe, to soothe; to satisfy (as hunger or thirst). *The small cups of water offered to the marathon runners helped to assuage their thirst.*

attenuate (ă·ˈten·yoo·ayt) *v.* 1. to make thin or slender 2. to weaken, reduce in force, value, or degree. *The Russian army was able to attenuate the strength and number of the German forces by leading them inland during winter.*

audacious (aw·ˈday·sh ŭs) *adj.* fearlessly or recklessly daring or bold; unrestrained by convention or propriety. *Detective Malloy's methods were considered bold and audacious by his superiors, and they often achieved results.*

august (aw·ˈgust) *adj.* majestic, venerable; inspiring admiration or reverence. *Jackie Kennedy's august dignity in the days following her husband's assassination set a tone for the rest of the nation as it mourned.*

auspice (ˈaw·spis) *n.* 1. protection or support, patronage 2. a forecast or omen. *The children's art museum was able to continue operating through the auspices of an anonymous wealthy benefactor.*

auspicious (aw·ˈspish·ŭs) *adj.* favorable, showing signs that promise success; propitious. *Valerie believed it an auspicious beginning when it rained on the day that she opened her umbrella store.*

austere (aw·ˈsteer) *adj.* 1. severe or stern in attitude or appearance 2. simple, unadorned, very plain. *With its simple but functional furniture and its obvious lack of decorative elements, the interior of the Shaker meeting hall was considered austere by many people.*

authoritarian (ă·thor·i·ˈtair·i·ăn) *adj.* favoring complete, unquestioning obedience to authority as opposed to individual freedom. *The military maintains an authoritarian environment for its officers and enlisted men alike.*

avant-garde (a·vahnt·ˈgahrd) *adj.* using or favoring an ultramodern or experimental style; innovative, cutting-edge, especially in the arts or literature. *Though it seems very conventional now, in the 1950's, Andy Warhol's art was viewed as avant-garde.*

aversion (ă·ˈvur·zhŏn) *n.* 1. a strong, intense dislike; repugnance 2. the object of this feeling. *Todd has an aversion to arugula and picks it out of his salads.*

baleful (ˈbayl·fŭl) *adj.* harmful, menacing, destructive, sinister. *Whether it's a man, woman, car, or animal, you can be certain to find at least one baleful character in a Stephen King horror novel.*

banal (bă·ˈnal) *adj.* commonplace, trite; obvious and uninteresting. *Though Tom and Susan had hoped for an adventure, they found that driving cross-country on the interstate offered mostly banal sites, restaurants, and attractions.*

bane (ˈbayn) *n.* 1. cause of trouble, misery, distress, or harm 2. poison. *The bane of the oak tree is the Asian beetle.*

beguile (bi·ˈgīl) *v.* to deceive or cheat through cunning; to distract the attention of, divert; to pass time in a pleasant manner, to amuse or charm. *Violet was able to beguile the spy, causing him to miss his secret meeting.*

belie (bi·ˈlī) *v.* 1. to give a false impression, misrepresent 2. to show to be false, to contradict. *By wearing an expensive suit and watch, Alan hoped to belie his lack of success to everyone at the reunion.*

bellicose (ˈbel·ĭ·kohs) *adj.* belligerent, quarrelsome, eager to make war. *There was little hope for peace following the election of a candidate known for his bellicose nature.*

belligerent (bi·ˈlij·ĕr·ĕnt) *adj.* hostile and aggressive, showing an eagerness to fight. *Ms. Rivera always kept an eye on Daniel during recess, as his belligerent attitude often caused problems with other children.*

bevy (ˈbev·ee) *n.* 1. a large group or assemblage 2. a flock of animals or birds. *There was a lively bevy of eager bingo fans waiting outside the bingo hall for the game to begin.*

bilk (bilk) *v.* to deceive or defraud; to swindle, cheat, especially to evade paying one's debts. *The stockbroker was led away in handcuffs, accused of trying to bilk senior citizens out of their investment dollars.*

blasphemy (ˈblas·fĕ·mee) *n.* contemptuous or irreverent acts, utterances, attitudes or writings against God or other things considered sacred; disrespect of something sacrosanct. *If you committed blasphemy during the Inquisition, you would be tortured and killed.*

blatant (ˈblay·tant) *adj.* completely obvious, not attempting to conceal in any way. *Samuel's blatant disregard of the rules earned him a two-week suspension.*

blight (blīt) *n.* 1. a plant disease that causes the affected parts to wilt and die 2. something that causes this condition, such as air pollution 3. something that impairs or destroys 4. an unsightly object or area. *They still do not know what caused the blight that destroyed half of the trees in the orchard.*

blithe (blīth) *adj.* light-hearted, casual, and carefree. *Rachel's blithe attitude toward spending money left her broke and in debt.*

boisterous (ˈboi·stĕ·rŭs) *adj.* 1. loud, noisy, and lacking restraint or discipline 2. stormy and rough. *The boisterous crowd began throwing cups onto the field during the football game.*

bolster (ˈbohl·stĕr) *v.* 1. to support or prop up 2. to buoy or hearten. *Coach Edmond's speech bolstered the team's confidence.*

bombastic (bom·ˈbas·tik) *adj.* speaking pompously, with inflated self-importance. *Ahmed was shocked that a renowned and admired humanitarian could give such a bombastic keynote address.*

boor (boor) *n.* a crude, offensive, ill-mannered person. *Seeing Chuck wipe his mouth with his sleeve, Maribel realized she was attending her senior prom with a classic boor.*

bourgeois (boor·ˈzhwah) *adj.* typical of the middle class; conforming to the standards and conventions of the middle class. *A house in the suburbs, two children, two cars, and three TVs are key indicators of a bourgeois lifestyle.*

bravado (bră·'vah·doh) *n.* false courage, a show of pretended bravery. *Kyle's bravado often got him in trouble with other kids in the neighborhood.*

broach (brohch) *v.* 1. to bring up, introduce, in order to begin a discussion of 2. to tap or pierce, as in to draw off liquid. *It was hard for Sarah to broach the subject of her mother's weight gain.*

bumptious ('bump·shŭs) *adj.* arrogant, conceited. *The bumptious man couldn't stop talking about himself or looking in the mirror.*

buoyant ('boi·ănt) *adj.* 1. able to float 2. light-hearted, cheerful. *In science class, the children tried to identify which objects on the table would be buoyant.*

burgeon ('bur·jŏn) *v.* to begin to grow and flourish; to begin to sprout, grow new buds, blossom. *The tulip bulbs beneath the soil would burgeon in early spring, providing there was no late frost.*

burnish ('bur·nish) *v.* to polish, rub to a shine. *When Kathryn began to burnish the old metal teapot, she realized that it was, in fact, solid silver.*

cabal (kă·'bal) *n.* 1. a scheme or conspiracy 2. a small group joined in a secret plot. *With Antonio as their leader, the members of the unit readied themselves to begin the coup.*

cadge (kaj) *v.* to beg, to obtain by begging. *Their dog Cleo would cadge at my feet, hoping I would throw him some table scraps.*

capricious (kă·'prish·ŭs) *adj.* impulsive, whimsical and unpredictable. *Robin Williams, the comedian, demonstrates a most capricious nature even when he is not performing.*

careen (kă·'reen) *v.* 1. to lurch from side to side while in motion 2. to rush carelessly or headlong. *Watching the car in front of us careen down the road was very frightening.*

caste (kast) *n.* a distinct social class or system. *While visiting India, Michael was fascinated to learn the particulars of each caste and the way they related to each other.*

castigate ('kas·tĭ·gayt) *v.* to inflict a severe punishment on; to chastise severely. *When she was caught stealing for the second time, Maya knew her mother would castigate her.*

catharsis (kă·'thahr·sis) *n.* the act of ridding or cleansing; relieving emotions via the experiences of others, especially through art. *Survivors of war often experience a catharsis when viewing Picasso's painting* Guernica, *which depicts the bombing of a town during the Spanish civil war.*

censure ('sen·shŭr) *n.* expression of strong criticism or disapproval; a rebuke or condemnation. *After the senator was found guilty of taking bribes, Congress unanimously agreed to censure him.*

chastise (chas·'tīz) *v.* to punish severely, as with a beating; to criticize harshly, rebuke. *Charles knew that his wife would chastise him after he inadvertently told the room full of guests that she had just had a facelift.*

chauvinist (ˈshoh·vĭn·ist) *n.* a person who believes in the superiority of his or her own kind; an extreme nationalist. *Though common in the early days of the women's movement, male chauvinists are pretty rare today.*

churlish (ˈchur·lĭsh) *adj.* ill-mannered, boorish, rude. *Angelo's churlish remarks made everyone at the table uncomfortable and ill at ease.*

circumspect (ˈsur·kŭm·spekt) *adj.* cautious, wary, watchful. *The captain was circumspect as she guided the boat through the fog.*

coeval (koh·ˈee·văl) *adj.* of the same time period, contemporary. *The growth of personal computers and CD players were coeval during the twentieth century.*

cogent (ˈkoh·jĕnt) *adj.* convincing, persuasive, compelling belief. *Ella's cogent arguments helped the debate team win the state championship.*

collusion (kŏ·ˈloo·zhŏn) *n.* a secret agreement between two or more people for a deceitful or fraudulent purpose; conspiracy. *The discovery of the e-mail proved that collusion existed between the CEO and CFO to defraud the shareholders.*

complaisant (kŏm·ˈplay·sănt) *adj.* tending to comply, obliging, willing to do what pleases others. *To preserve family peace and harmony, Lenny became very complaisant when his in-laws came to visit.*

conciliatory (kŏn·ˈsil·i·ă·tohr·ee) *adj.* making or willing to make concessions to reconcile, soothe, or comfort; mollifying, appeasing. *Abraham Lincoln made conciliatory gestures toward the South at the end of the Civil War.*

conclave (ˈkon·klav) *n.* a private or secret meeting. *The double agent had a conclave with the spy he was supposed to be observing.*

consternation (kon·stĕr·ˈnay·shŏn) *n.* a feeling of deep, incapacitating horror or dismay. *The look of consternation on the faces of the students taking the history exam alarmed the teacher, who thought he had prepared his students for the test.*

contentious (kŏn·ˈten·shŭs) *adj.* 1. quarrelsome, competitive, quick to fight 2. controversial, causing contention. *With two contentious candidates on hand, it was sure to be a lively debate.*

conundrum (kŏ·ˈnun·drŭm) *n.* a hard riddle, enigma; a puzzling question or problem. *Alex's logic professor gave the class a conundrum to work on over the weekend.*

cornucopia (kor·nyŭ·ˈkoh·pi·ă) *n.* abundance; a horn of plenty. *The first-graders made cornucopias for Thanksgiving by placing papier-mache vegetables into a hollowed-out horn.*

countenance (ˈkown·tĕ·năns) *n.* the appearance of a person's face, facial features and expression. *As she walked down the aisle, Julia's countenance was absolutely radiant.*

craven (ˈkray·vĕn) *adj.* cowardly. *"This craven act of violence will not go unpunished," remarked the police chief.*

credulous (ˈkrej·ŭ·lŭs) *adj.* gullible, too willing to believe things. *All the tables, graphs, and charts made the company's assets look too good to the credulous potential investors at the meeting.*

daunt (dawnt) *v.* to intimidate, to make afraid or discouraged. *Members of the opposing team were trying to daunt the home team by yelling loudly and beating their chests.*

de facto (dee ˈfak·toh) *adj.* in reality or fact; actual. *Though there was a ceremonial head of government, General Ashtononi was the de facto leader of the country.*

debacle (di·ˈbah·kĕl) *n.* 1. a sudden disaster or collapse; a total defeat or failure 2. a sudden breaking up or breaking loose; violent flood waters, often caused by the breaking up of ice in a river. *Putting the bridge's supporting beams in loose sand caused a total debacle when the sand shifted and the bridge fell apart.*

decimate (ˈdes·ĭ·mayt) *v.* to destroy a large portion of. *Neglect and time would eventually decimate much of the housing in the inner cities.*

decorum (di·ˈkohr·ŭm) *n.* appropriateness of behavior, propriety; decency in manners and conduct. *When questions concerning decorum arise, I always refer to Emily Post.*

deign (dayn) *v.* to condescend, to be kind or gracious enough to do something thought to be beneath one's dignity. *Would you deign to spare a dime for a poor old beggar like me?*

delineate (di·ˈlin·i·ayt) *v.* to draw or outline, sketch; to portray, depict, describe. *The survey will clearly delineate where their property ends.*

demagogue (ˈdem·ă·gawg) *n.* a leader who obtains power by appealing to people's feelings and prejudices rather than by reasoning. *Hilter was the most infamous demagogue of the twentieth century.*

demur (di·ˈmur) *v.* to raise objections, hesitate. *Polly hated to demur, but she didn't think adding ten cloves of garlic to the recipe would make it taste good.*

demure (di·ˈmyoor) *adj.* modest and shy, or pretending to be so. *When it was to her advantage, Sharon could be very demure, but otherwise she was quite outgoing.*

denigrate (ˈden·i·grayt) *v.* to blacken the reputation of, disparage, defame. *The movie script reportedly contained scenes that would denigrate the Queen, so those scenes were removed.*

denouement (day·noo·ˈmahn) *n.* the resolution or clearing up of the plot at the end of a narrative; the outcome or solution of an often complex series of events. *The students sat at the edge of their seats as they listened to the denouement of the story.*

deprecate (ˈdep·rĕ·kayt) *v.* to express disapproval of; to belittle, depreciate. *Grandpa's tendency to deprecate the children's friends was a frequent source of family strife.*

derisive (di·ˈrī·siv) *adj.* scornful, expressing ridicule; mocking, jeering. *In order to promote freedom of expression, derisive comments were forbidden in the classroom.*

derivative (di·ʹriv·ă·tiv) *adj.* derived from another source, unoriginal. *The word "atomic" is a derivative of the word "atom."*

desecrate (ʹdes·ĕ·krayt) *v.* to violate the sacredness of, to profane. *Someone desecrated the local cemetery by spray-painting graffiti on tombstones.*

desultory (ʹdes·ŭl·tohr·ee) *adj.* aimless, haphazard; moving from one subject to another without logical connection. *The family became concerned listening to Steven's desultory ramblings.*

dichotomy (dī·ʹkot·ŏ·mee) *n.* division into two usually contradictory parts or kinds. *When the teacher broached the subject of the election, there was a predictable dichotomy among the students.*

diffident (ʹdif·i·dĕnt) *adj.* lacking self-confidence, shy and timid. *Alan's diffident nature is often misinterpreted as arrogance.*

dilatory (ʹdil·ă·tohr·ee) *adj.* slow or late in doing something; intended to delay, especially to gain time. *Resentful for having to work the holiday, Miguel's dilatory approach to getting himself up and dressed was his own small act of passive resistance.*

disabuse (dis·ă·ʹbyooz) *v.* to undeceive, correct a false impression or erroneous belief. *Natalie needed to disabuse Chin of his belief that she was in love with him.*

disconcert (dis·kŏn·ʹsurt) *v.* 1. to upset the composure of, ruffle 2. to frustrate plans by throwing into disorder. *The arrival of Miriam's ex-husband and his new wife managed to disconcert the typically unflappable Miriam.*

disconsolate (dis·ʹkon·sŏ·lit) *adj.* 1. sad, dejected, disappointed 2. inconsolable, hopelessly unhappy. *The disconsolate look on Peter's face revealed that the letter contained bad news.*

disenfranchise (dis·en·ʹfran·chīz) *v.* to deprive of the rights of citizenship, especially the right to vote. *The independent monitors were at polling locations to ensure neither party tried to disenfranchise incoming voters.*

disingenuous (dis·in·ʹjen·yoo·ŭs) *adj.* 1. insincere, calculating; not straightforward or frank 2. falsely pretending to be unaware. *Carl's disingenuous comments were not taken seriously by anyone in the room.*

disparage (di·ʹspar·ij) *v.* to speak of in a slighting or derogatory way, belittle. *Comedians often disparage politicians as part of their comedic routines.*

dissemble (di·ʹsem·bĕl) *v.* to disguise or conceal one's true feelings or motives behind a false appearance. *Tom needed to dissemble his desire for his boss's job by acting supportive of her planned job change.*

dissuade (di·ʹswayd) *v.* to discourage from or persuade against a course of action. *I tried to dissuade them from painting their house purple, but they didn't listen.*

dither (ʹdith·ĕr) *v.* 1. to hesitate, be indecisive and uncertain 2. to shake or quiver. *During a crisis, it is important to have a leader who will not dither.*

dogma ('dawg·mă) *n.* a system of principles or beliefs, a prescribed doctrine. *Some find the dogma inherent in religion a comfort, whereas others find it too restrictive.*

dogmatic (dawg·'mat·ik) *adj.* 1. asserting something in a positive, absolute, arrogant way 2. of or relating to dogma. *His dogmatic style of conversation was not very popular with his young students.*

dross (draws) *n.* 1. waste product, sludge 2. something worthless, commonplace, or trivial. *Work crews immediately began the task of cleaning the dross at the abandoned plastics factory.*

dulcet ('dul·sit) *adj.* melodious, harmonious, sweet-sounding. *The chamber orchestra's dulcet tunes were a perfect ending to a great evening.*

ebullient (i·'bul·yĕnt) *adj.* bubbling over with enthusiasm, exuberant. *The ebullient children were waiting to stick their hands into the grab bag and pull out a toy.*

éclat (ay·'klah) *n.* conspicuous success; great acclaim or applause; brilliant performance or achievement. *Even the ruinous deceit of the envious Salieri could not impede the dazzling éclat of the young and gifted Mozart.*

edifying ('ed·ĭ·fī·ing) *adj.* enlightening or uplifting with the aim of improving intellectual or moral development; instructing, improving. *His edifying sermon challenged the congregation to devote more time to charitable causes.*

efficacious (ef·ĭ·'kay·shŭs) *adj.* acting effectively, producing the desired effect or result. *Margaret's efficacious approach to her job in the collections department made her a favorite with the CFO.*

effrontery (i·'frun·tĕ·ree) *n.* brazen boldness, impudence, insolence. *The customs officials were infuriated by the effrontery of the man who nonchalantly carried drugs into the country in his shirt pocket.*

effusive (i·'fyoo·siv) *adj.* expressing emotions in an unrestrained or excessive way; profuse, overflowing, gushy. *Anne's unexpectedly effusive greeting made Tammy uncomfortable.*

egalitarian (i·gal·i·'tair·i·ăn) *adj.* characterized by or affirming the principle of equal political, social, civil, and economic rights for all persons. *Hannah was moved by the candidate's egalitarian speech.*

eke (eek) *v.* to get or supplement with great effort or strain; to earn or accomplish laboriously. *Working two jobs enabled Quincy to eke out a living wage for his family.*

élan (ay·'lahn) *n.* 1. vivacity, enthusiasm, vigor 2. distinctive style or flair. *The new designer's élan and originality was sure to help him succeed in the highly competitive fashion industry.*

elite (i·'leet) *n.* 1. the best or most skilled members of a social group or class 2. a person or group regarded as superior. *Within the student orchestra, there existed a small group of musical elite who performed around the country.*

eloquent ('el·ŏ·kwĕnt) *adj.* expressing strong emotions or arguments in a powerful, fluent, and persuasive manner. *Abraham Lincoln's Gettysburg Address is considered one of the most eloquent speeches ever given by a U.S. president.*

eminent ('em·ĭ·nĕnt) *adj.* towering above or more prominent than others, lofty; standing above others in quality, character, reputation, etc.; distinguished. *The chairperson proudly announced that the keynote speaker at the animal rights convention would be the eminent primatologist Jane Goodall.*

empirical (em·'pir·i·kal) *adj.* based on observation or experience rather than theory. *Frank's empirical data suggested that mice would climb over the walls of the maze to get to the cheese rather than navigate the maze itself.*

enclave ('en·klayv) *n.* a distinct territory lying wholly within the boundaries of another, larger territory. *The country of Lesotho is an enclave of South Africa.*

endemic (en·'dem·ik) *adj.* 1. prevalent in or characteristic of a specific area or group of people 2. native to a particular region. *Kudzu, a hairy, purple-flowered vine thought to be endemic to the southeastern United States, was actually imported from Japan.*

enervate ('en·ĕr·vayt) *v.* to weaken, deprive of strength or vitality; to make feeble or impotent. *Stephanie's cutting remarks managed to enervate Hasaan.*

engender (en·'jen·dĕr) *v.* to produce, give rise to, bring into existence. *Professor Sorenson's support worked to engender Samantha's desire to pursue a Ph.D.*

enigma (ĕ·'nig·mă) *n.* 1. something that is puzzling or difficult to understand; a perplexing or inexplicable thing that cannot be explained 2. a baffling problem or difficult riddle. *How Winston came to be the president of this organization is a true enigma.*

enormity (i·'nor·mi·tee) *n.* 1. excessive wickedness 2. a monstrous offense or evil act, atrocity. (*Note:* Enormity is often used to indicate something of great size (e.g., the enormity of the task), but this is considered an incorrect use of the word.) *The enormity of Jeffery Dahmer's crimes will never be forgotten.*

ephemeral (i·'fem·ĕ·răl) *adj.* lasting only a very short time, transitory. *Numerous ephemeral ponds and pools can be found in the desert during the rainy season.*

epicurean (ep·i·'kyoor·i·ăn) *n.* a person devoted to the pursuit of pleasure and luxury, especially the enjoyment of good food and comfort. *While on vacation at a posh resort hotel, Joan became a true epicurean.*

epitome (i·'pit·ŏ·mee) *n.* 1. something or someone that embodies a particular quality or characteristic, a representative example or a typical model 2. a brief summary or abstract. *With his ten-gallon hat, western shirt, and rugged jeans, Alex was the epitome of the American cowboy.*

equanimity (ee·kwă·'nim·i·tee) *n.* calmness of temperament, even-temperedness; patience and composure, especially under stressful circumstances. *The hostage negotiator's equanimity during the standoff was remarkable.*

equivocate (i·'kwiv·ŏ·kayt) *v.* to use unclear or ambiguous language in order to mislead or conceal the truth. *Raj tried to equivocate when explaining why he came home after his curfew.*

eradicate (i·ˈrad·ĭ·kayt) *v.* to root out and utterly destroy; to annihilate, exterminate. *The exterminator said he would eradicate the vermin from the house.*

erratic (i·ˈrat·ik) *adj.* 1. moving or behaving in an irregular, uneven, or inconsistent manner 2. deviating from the normal or typical course of action, opinion, etc. *During an earthquake, a seismograph's needle moves in an erratic manner.*

erudite (ˈer·yŭ·dīt) *adj.* having or showing great learning; profoundly educated, scholarly. *The scholarly work of nonfiction was obviously written by an erudite young author.*

ethos (ˈee·thos) *n.* the spirit, attitude, disposition or beliefs characteristic of a community, epoch, region, etc. *The ethos of their group included a commitment to pacifism.*

eulogy (ˈyoo·lŏ·gee) *n.* a formal speech or piece of writing in praise of someone or something. *Richard was asked to give a eulogy for his fallen comrade.*

euphoria (yoo·ˈfohr·i·ă) *n.* a feeling of well-being or high spirits. *When falling in love, it is not uncommon to experience feelings of euphoria.*

evince (i·ˈvins) *v.* to show or demonstrate clearly; to make evident. *The safety officer tried to evince the dangers of driving under the influence by showing pictures of alcohol-related automobile accidents.*

exacerbate (ig·ˈzas·ĕr·bayt) *v.* to make worse; to increase the severity, violence, or bitterness of. *We should have known that splashing salt water on Dan's wound would exacerbate his pain.*

exculpate (eks·ˈkul·payt) *v.* to free from blame, to clear from a charge of guilt. *When Anthony admitted to the crime, it served to exculpate Marcus.*

exigent (ˈek·si·jĕnt) *adj.* 1. urgent, requiring immediate action or attention, critical 2. requiring much effort or precision, demanding. *The late-night call on Paul's cell phone concerned matters of an exigent nature.*

exorbitant (ig·ˈzor·bi·tănt) *adj.* greatly exceeding the bounds of what is normal or reasonable; inordinate and excessive. *Three thousand dollars is an exorbitant amount to pay for a scarf.*

expedient (ik·ˈspee·di·ĕnt) *adj.* 1. appropriate for a purpose, a suitable means to an end 2. serving to promote one's own interests rather than principle. *A quick divorce was an expedient end to the couple's two-month marriage.*

expunge (ik·ˈspunj) *v.* to wipe or rub out, delete; to eliminate completely, annihilate. *After finishing probation, juveniles can petition the courts to expunge their criminal records.*

extenuate (ik·ˈsten·yoo·ayt) *v.* to reduce the strength or lessen the seriousness of, to try to partially excuse. *Fred claimed that extenuating circumstances forced him to commit forgery.*

facetious (fă·ˈsee·shŭs) *adj.* humorous and witty, cleverly amusing; jocular, sportive. *Ms. Weston's facetious remarks always made people laugh.*

fatuous ('fach·oo·ŭs) *adj.* complacently stupid; feeble-minded and silly. *Since Sam was such an intellectually accomplished student, Mr. Britt was surprised to discover that Sam's well-meaning but fatuous parents were not at all like him.*

feckless ('fek·lis) *adj.* 1. lacking purpose or vitality; feeble, weak 2. incompetent and ineffective, careless. *Jake's feckless performance led to his termination from the team.*

fecund ('fek·ŭnd) *adj.* fertile. *The fecund soil in the valley was able to sustain the growing community.*

feign (fayn) *v.* to pretend, to give the false appearance of. *Walter feigned illness to avoid attending the meeting.*

felicitous (fi·'lis·i·tŭs) *adj.* 1. apt, suitably expressed, apropos 2. marked by good fortune. *The felicitous turn of events during her promotional tour propelled Susan's book to the bestseller list.*

fervent ('fur·vĕnt) *adj.* 1. having or showing great emotion; ardent, zealous 2. extremely hot, burning. *Norman had a fervent belief that aliens had already landed on earth.*

fervor ('fur·vŏr) *n.* zeal, ardor, intense emotion. *The fervor of the fans in the stands helped propel the team to victory.*

fetter ('fet·ĕr) *v.* 1. to shackle, put in chains 2. to impede or restrict. *The presence of two security guards fettered their plans to get backstage.*

flaccid ('flak·sid) *adj.* hanging loose or wrinkled; weak, flabby, not firm. *The skin of cadavers becomes flaccid in a matter of hours.*

flippant ('flip·ănt) *adj.* not showing proper seriousness; disrespectful, saucy. *Ursula's flippant remarks in front of her fiancé's parents were an embarrassment to us all.*

florid ('flor·id) *adj.* 1. elaborate, ornate 2. (of complexion) ruddy, rosy. *The florid architecture in Venice did not appeal to me; I prefer buildings without so much ornamentation.*

flout (flowt) *v.* to disobey openly and scornfully; to reject, mock, go against (as in a tradition or convention). *Flappers in the early 20th century would flout convention by bobbing their hair and wearing very short skirts.*

forbearance (for·'bair·ăns) *n.* patience, willingness to wait, tolerance. *Gustaf dreaded the security check in the airport, but he faced it with great forbearance because he knew it was for his own safety.*

forestall (fohr·'stawl) *v.* to prevent by taking action first, preempt. *The diplomat was able to forestall a conflict by holding secret meetings with both parties.*

forswear (for·'swair) *v.* 1. to give up, renounce 2. to deny under oath. *Natasha had to forswear her allegiance to her homeland in order to become a citizen of the new country.*

frugal ('froo·găl) *adj.* 1. careful and economical, sparing, thrifty 2. costing little. *My grandparents survived the Great Depression by being very frugal.*

fulminate ('ful·mĭ·nayt) *v.* 1. to issue a thunderous verbal attack, berate 2. to explode or detonate. *The senator was prone to fulminating when other legislators questioned her ideology.*

fulsome ('fuul·sŏm) *adj.* offensive due to excessiveness, especially excess flattery or praise. *Her new coworker's fulsome attention bothered Malinda.*

gainsay ('gayn·say) *v.* to deny, contradict, or declare false; to oppose. *Petra would gainsay all accusations made against her.*

gargantuan (gahr·'gan·choo·ăn) *adj.* gigantic, huge. *It was a gargantuan supermarket for such a small town.*

garish ('gair·ish) *adj.* excessively bright or overdecorated, gaudy; tastelessly showy. *Though Susan thought Las Vegas was garish, Emily thought it was perfectly beautiful.*

garrulous ('gar·ŭ·lŭs) *adj.* talkative. *Andrew had the unfortunate luck of being seated next to a garrulous young woman for his 12-hour flight.*

genteel (jen·'teel) *adj.* elegantly polite, well-bred, refined. *The genteel host made sure that each entrée was cooked to each guest's specifications.*

gregarious (grĕ·'gair·i·ŭs) *adj.* 1. seeking and enjoying the company of others, sociable 2. tending to form a group with others of the same kind. *John was a gregarious fellow who always had fun at social events.*

guffaw (gu·'faw) *n.* a noisy, coarse burst of laughter. *Michael let out quite a guffaw when Jamal told him the outlandish joke.*

guile (gīl) *n.* treacherous cunning; shrewd, crafty deceit. *The most infamous pirates displayed tremendous guile.*

hallow ('hal·oh) *v.* to make holy, consecrate. *The religious leader proclaimed the new worship hall a hallowed space.*

hapless ('hap·lis) *adj.* unlucky, unfortunate. *The hapless circumstances of her journey resulted in lost luggage, missed connections, and a very late arrival.*

harangue (hă·'rang) *n.* a long, often scolding or bombastic speech; a tirade. *Members of the audience began to get restless during the senator's political harangue.*

harbinger ('hahr·bin·jĕr) *n.* a person, thing, or event that foreshadows or indicates what is to come; a forerunner or precursor. *The arrival of the robins is a harbinger of spring.*

harrowing ('har·oh·ing) *adj.* distressing, creating great stress or torment. *The turbulent flight proved to be a harrowing experience for Jane.*

haughty ('haw·tee) *adj.* scornfully arrogant and condescending; acting as though one is superior and others unworthy, disdainful. *Stanley is so often haughty that he has very few friends.*

hegemony (hi·ˈjem·ŏ·nee) *n.* predominant influence or leadership, especially of one government over others. *A military takeover in the impoverished country secured the hegemony of the Centrist Party in its bid for power.*

hermetic (hur·ˈmet·ik) *adj.* having an airtight closure; protected from outside influences. *Astronauts go for space walks only when wearing hermetic space suits.*

iconoclast (ī·ˈkon·oh·klast) *n.* 1. a person who attacks and seeks to overthrow traditional ideas, beliefs, or institutions 2. someone who opposes and destroys idols used in worship. *Using words as weapons, the well-spoken iconoclast challenged religious hypocrisy and fanaticism wherever she found it.*

ignoble (ig·ˈnoh·bĕl) *adj.* 1. lacking nobility in character or purpose, dishonorable 2. not of the nobility, common. *Mark was an ignoble successor to such a well-respected leader, and many members of the organization resigned.*

ignominious (ig·nŏ·ˈmin·i·ŭs) *adj.* 1. marked by shame or disgrace 2. deserving disgrace or shame; despicable. *The evidence of plagiarism brought an ignominious end to what had been a notable career for the talented young author.*

imbroglio (im·ˈbrohl·yoh) *n.* a confused or difficult situation, usually involving disagreement. *An imbroglio developed when the bus drivers went on strike, leaving thousands of commuters stranded at the bus station with no way to get home.*

immolate (ˈim·ŏ·layt) *v.* 1. to kill, as a sacrifice 2. to kill (oneself) by fire 3. to destroy (one thing for another). *It was a tragic end to the protester's life when, out of desperation, he decided to immolate himself in public.*

impasse (ˈim·pas) *n.* a deadlock, stalemate; a difficulty without a solution. *The labor negotiations with management reached an impasse, and a strike seemed imminent.*

impassive (im·ˈpas·iv) *adj.* not showing or feeling emotion or pain. *It was hard to know what she was feeling by looking at the impassive expression on her face.*

impecunious (im·pĕ·ˈkyoo·ni·ŭs) *adj.* having little or no money; poor, penniless. *Many impecunious immigrants to the United States eventually were able to make comfortable lives for themselves.*

imperialism (im·ˈpeer·i·ă·liz·ĕm) *n.* the policy of extending the rule or authority of a nation or empire by acquiring other territories or dependencies. *Great Britain embraced imperialism, acquiring so many territories that the sun never set on the British Empire.*

imperious (im·ˈpeer·i·ŭs) *adj.* overbearing, bossy, domineering. *Stella was relieved with her new job transfer because she would no longer be under the control of such an imperious boss.*

impetuous (im·ˈpech·oo·ŭs) *adj.* 1. characterized by sudden, forceful energy or emotion; impulsive, unduly hasty and without thought 2. marked by violent force. *It was an impetuous decision to run off to Las Vegas and get married after a one-week courtship.*

implacable (im-ˈplak-ă-bĕl) *adj.* incapable of being placated or appeased; inexorable. *Some of the people who call the customer service desk for assistance are implacable, but most are relatively easy to serve.*

importune (im-por-ˈtoon) *v.* 1. to ask incessantly, make incessant requests 2. to beg persistently and urgently. *Children can't help but importune during the holidays, constantly nagging for the irresistible toys they see advertised on television.*

imprecation (im-prĕ-ˈkay-shŏn) *n.* an invocation of evil, a curse. *In the book I'm reading, the gypsy queen levies an imprecation on the lead character.*

impudent (ˈim-pyŭ-dĕnt) *adj.* 1. boldly showing a lack of respect, insolent 2. shamelessly forward, immodest. *Thumbing his nose at the principal was an impudent act.*

impute (im-ˈpyoot) *v.* to attribute to a cause or source, ascribe, credit. *Doctors impute the reduction in cancer deaths to the nationwide decrease in cigarette smoking.*

incendiary (in-ˈsen-di-er-ee) *adj.* 1. causing or capable of causing fire; burning readily 2. of or involving arson 3. tending to incite or inflame, inflammatory. *Fire marshals checked for incendiary devices in the theater after they received an anonymous warning.*

inchoate (in-ˈkoh-it) *adj.* 1. just begun; in an initial or early stage of development, incipient 2. not yet fully formed, undeveloped, incomplete. *During the inchoate stage of fetal growth, it is difficult to distinguish between a cow, a frog, and a human; as they mature, the developing embryos take on the characteristics of their own particular species.*

incredulous (in-ˈkrej-ŭ-lŭs) *adj.* skeptical, unwilling to believe. (*Note:* Do not confuse with *incredible*, meaning "implausible or beyond belief.") *The members of the jury were incredulous when they heard the defendant's farfetched explanation of the crime.*

incursion (in-ˈkur-zhŏn) *n.* a raid or temporary invasion of someone else's territory; the act of entering or running into a territory or domain. *There was an incursion on the western border of their country.*

indefatigable (in-di-ˈfat-ĭ-gă-bĕl) *adj.* not easily exhausted or fatigued; tireless. *The indefatigability of the suffragette movement led to the passage of the 20th Amendment, guaranteeing women the right to vote.*

indolent (ˈin-dŏ-lĕnt) *adj.* 1. lazy, lethargic, inclined to avoid labor 2. causing little or no pain; slow to grow or heal. *Iris's indolent attitude did not bode well for her professional future.*

indomitable (in-ˈdom-i-tă-bĕl) *adj.* not able to be vanquished or overcome, unconquerable; not easily discouraged or subdued. *The indomitable spirit of the Olympic athletes was inspirational.*

ineluctable (in-i-ˈluk-tă-bĕl) *adj.* certain, inevitable; not to be avoided or overcome. *The ineluctable outcome of the two-person race was that there would be one winner and one loser.*

infidel ('in·fi·dĕl) *n.* 1. a person with no religious beliefs 2. a nonbeliever, one who does not accept a particular religion, doctrine, or system of beliefs. *Because Tom had been raised with strict religious beliefs, it was no surprise that he was viewed as a heathen and an infidel by his family when he refused to be married in the church.*

ingenuous (in·'jen·yoo·ŭs) *adj.* 1. not cunning or deceitful, unable to mask feelings; artless, frank, sincere 2. lacking sophistication or worldliness. (*Note:* Do not confuse with *ingenious*, meaning "remarkably clever.") *Don's expression of regret was ingenuous, for even though he didn't know her well, he felt a deep sadness when Mary died.*

inimitable (i·'nim·i·tă·bĕl) *adj.* defying imitation, unmatchable. *His performance on the tennis court was inimitable, and he won three championships.*

inscrutable (in·'scroo·tă·bĕl) *adj.* baffling, unfathomable, incapable of being understood. *It was completely inscrutable how the escape artist got out of the trunk.*

insolent ('in·sŏ·lĕnt) *adj.* haughty and contemptuous; brazen, disrespectful, impertinent. *Parents of teenagers often observe the insolent behavior that typically accompanies adolescence.*

insouciant (in·'soo·si·ănt) *adj.* unconcerned, carefree, indifferent. *Wendy's insouciant attitude toward her future concerned her father, who expected her to go to college.*

interdict (in·tĕr·'dikt) *v.* to prohibit, forbid. *Carlos argued that the agriculture department should interdict plans to produce genetically modified foods.*

intractable (in·'trak·tă·bĕl) *adj.* unmanageable, unruly, stubborn. *The young colt was intractable, and training had to be cancelled temporarily.*

intransigent (in·'tran·si·jĕnt) *adj.* unwilling to compromise, stubborn. *Young children can be intransigent when it comes to what foods they will eat, insisting on familiar favorites and rejecting anything new.*

intrepid (in·'trep·id) *adj.* fearless, brave, undaunted. *The intrepid nature and fortitude of the U.S. Marines is legendary.*

inured (in·'yoord) *adj.* accustomed to, adapted. *Trisha had become inured to her boss's criticism, and it no longer bothered her.*

inveigle (in·'vay·gĕl) *v.* 1. to influence or persuade through gentle coaxing or flattery; to entice. *Vanessa inveigled her way into a promotion that should have gone to Marie.*

inveterate (in·'vet·ĕ·rit) *adj.* habitual; deep rooted, firmly established. *I am an inveterate pacifist and am unlikely to change my mind.*

involute ('in·vŏ·loot) *adj.* intricate, complex. *The tax reform committee faces an extremely involute problem if it wants to distribute the tax burden equally.*

iota (ī·'oh·tă) *n.* a very small amount; the smallest possible quantity. *Professor Carlton is so unpopular because he doesn't have one iota of respect for his students.*

irascible (i·ˈras·ĭ·bĕl) *adj.* irritable, easily aroused to anger, hot tempered. *Her irascible temperament caused many problems with the staff at the office.*

ire (īr) *n.* anger, wrath. *I was filled with ire when Vladimir tried to take credit for my work.*

irk (urk) *v.* to annoy, irritate, vex. *Being a teenager means being continually irked by your parents—and vice versa.*

irresolute (i·ˈrez·ŏ·loot) *adj.* feeling or showing uncertainty; hesitant, indecisive. *Sandra is still irresolute, so if you talk to her, you might help her make up her mind.*

jocund (ˈjok·ŭnd) *adj.* merry, cheerful; sprightly and lighthearted. *Alexi's jocund nature makes it a pleasure to be near her.*

laconic (lă·ˈkon·ik) *adj.* brief, to the point, terse. *Morrison's ten-minute commencement address was everything we could have asked for: laconic, powerful, and inspirational.*

laissez-faire (les·ay ˈfair) *adj.* hands-off policy; noninterference by the government in business and economic affairs. *I believe a more laissez-faire approach by management would make everyone more cooperative and productive.*

libertine (ˈlib·ĕr·teen) *n.* one who lives or acts in an immoral or irresponsible way; one who acts according to his or her own impulses and desires and is unrestrained by conventions or morals. *They claim to be avant-garde, but in my opinion, they're just a bunch of libertines.*

lilliputian (lil·i·ˈpyoo·shăn) *adj.* 1. very small, tiny 2. trivial or petty. *My troubles are lilliputian compared to hers, and I am thankful that I do not have such major issues in my life.*

loquacious (loh·ˈkway·shŭs) *adj.* talkative, garrulous. *The loquacious woman sitting next to me on the six-hour bus ride talked the entire time.*

lucid (ˈloo·sid) *adj.* 1. very clear, easy to understand, intelligible 2. sane or rational. *Andrea presented a very lucid argument that proved her point beyond a shadow of a doubt.*

lucrative (ˈloo·kră·tiv) *adj.* profitable, producing much money. *Teaching is a very rewarding career, but unfortunately it is not very lucrative.*

lugubrious (luu·ˈgoo·bri·ŭs) *adj.* excessively dismal or mournful, often exaggeratedly or ridiculously so. *Billy looks like a fool, acting so lugubrious over losing a silly bet.*

maladroit (mal·ă·ˈdroit) *adj.* clumsy, bungling, inept. *The maladroit waiter broke a dozen plates and spilled coffee on two customers.*

malaise (mă·ˈlayz) *n.* a feeling of illness or unease. *After his malaise persisted for more than a week, Nicholas went to see a doctor.*

malapropism (ˈmal·ă·prop·iz·ĕm) *n.* comical misuse of words, especially those that are similar in sound. *His malapropisms may make us laugh, but they won't win our vote.*

malfeasance (măl·ʹfee·zăns) *n.* misconduct or wrongdoing, especially by a public official; improper professional conduct. *The city comptroller was found guilty of malfeasance and removed from office.*

malinger (mă·ʹling·gĕr) *v.* to pretend to be injured or ill in order to avoid work. *Stop malingering and give me a hand with this job.*

malleable (ʹmal·i·ă·bĕl) *adj.* 1. easily molded or pressed into shape 2. easily controlled or influenced 3. easily adapting to changing circumstances. *You should be able to convince Xiu quickly; she's quite a malleable person.*

maverick (ʹmav·ĕr·ik) *n.* rebel, nonconformist, one who acts independently. *Madonna has always been a maverick in the music industry.*

mélange (may·ʹlahnzh) *n.* a mixture or assortment. *There was a very interesting mélange of people at the party.*

mellifluous (me·ʹlif·loo·ŭs) *adj.* sounding sweet and flowing; honeyed. *Her mellifluous voice floated in through the windows and made everyone smile.*

mendacity (men·ʹdas·i·tee) *n.* 1. the tendency to be dishonest or untruthful 2. a falsehood or lie. *Carlos's mendacity has made him very unpopular with his classmates, who don't feel they can trust him.*

mercurial (mĕr·ʹkyoor·i·ăl) *adj.* 1. liable to change moods suddenly 2. lively, changeable, volatile. *Fiona is so mercurial that you never know what kind of reaction to expect.*

meretricious (mer·ĕ·ʹtrish·ŭs) *adj.* gaudy, tawdry; showily attractive but false or insincere. *With its casinos and attractions, some people consider Las Vegas the most meretricious city in the country.*

mete (meet) *v.* to distribute, allot, apportion. *The punishments were meted out fairly to everyone involved in the plot.*

mettlesome (ʹmet·ĕl·sŏm) *adj.* courageous, high-spirited. (*Note:* Do not confuse with *meddlesome*, meaning "inclined to interfere.") *Alice's mettlesome attitude was infectious and inspired us all to press on.*

mince (mins) *v.* 1. to cut into very small pieces 2. to walk or speak affectedly, as with studied refinement 3. to say something more delicately or indirectly for the sake of politeness or decorum. *Please don't mince your words—just tell me what you want to say.*

minutiae (mi·ʹnoo·shi·ee) *n., pl.* very small details; trivial or trifling matters. *His attention to the minutiae of the process enabled him to make his great discovery.*

mirth (murth) *n.* great merriment, joyous laughter. *The joyous wedding celebration filled the reception hall with mirth throughout the evening.*

misanthrope (mis·ʹan·throhp) *n.* one who hates or distrusts humankind. *Pay no mind to his criticism; he's a real misanthrope, and no one can do anything right in his eyes.*

miscreant ('mis·kree·ănt) *n.* a villain, criminal; evil person. *The miscreant had eluded the police for months, but today he was finally captured.*

mitigate ('mit·ĭ·gayt) *v.* 1. to make less intense or severe 2. to moderate the force or intensity of, soften, diminish, alleviate. *The unusual extenuating circumstances mitigated her punishment.*

mollify ('mol·ĭ·fī) *v.* 1. to soothe the anger of, calm 2. to lessen in intensity 3. to soften, make less rigid. *The crying child was quickly mollified by her mother.*

moot (moot) *adj.* debatable, undecided. *Although this is a moot issue, it is one that is often debated among certain circles.*

morose (mŏ·'rohs) *adj.* gloomy, sullen, melancholy. *My daughter has been morose ever since our dog ran away.*

multifarious (mul·ti·'fair·i·ŭs) *adj.* very varied, greatly diversified; having many aspects. *The job requires the ability to handle multifarious tasks.*

mundane (mun·'dayn) *adj.* 1. dull, routine; commonplace, ordinary 2. worldly as opposed to spiritual. *My job may be mundane, but it is secure and it pays well.*

nadir ('nay·dĭr) *n.* the very bottom, the lowest point. *When he felt he was at the nadir of his life, Robert began to practice mediation to elevate his spirits.*

narcissism ('narh·si·siz·ĕm) *n.* admiration or worship of oneself; excessive interest in one's own personal features. *Some critics say that movie stars are guilty of narcissism.*

nascent ('nas·ĕnt) *adj.* coming into existence, emerging. *The nascent movement gathered strength quickly and soon became a nationwide call to action.*

nemesis ('nem·ĕ·sis) *n.* 1. source of harm or ruin, the cause of one's misery or downfall; bane 2. agent of retribution or vengeance. *In "Frankenstein," the monster Victor creates becomes his nemesis.*

nexus ('nek·sŭs) *n.* 1. a means of connection, a link or tie between a series of things 2. a connected series or group 3. the core or center. *The nexus between the lobbyists and the recent policy changes is clear.*

noisome ('noi·sŏm) *adj.* 1. offensive, foul, especially in odor; putrid 2. harmful, noxious. *What a noisome odor is coming from that garbage can!*

non sequitur (non 'sek·wi·tŭr) *n.* a conclusion that does not logically follow from the evidence. *Marcus's argument started off strong, but it degenerated into a series of non sequiturs.*

nonchalant (non·shă·'lahnt) *adj.* indifferent or cool, not showing anxiety or excitement. *Victoria tried to be nonchalant, but I could tell she was nervous.*

noxious ('nok·shŭs) *adj.* unpleasant and harmful, unwholesome. *The noxious smell drove everyone from the room.*

nullify ('nul·ĭ·fī) *v.* 1. to make null (without legal force), invalidate 2. to counteract or neutralize the effect of. *The opponents wanted to nullify the bill before it became a law.*

obdurate ('ob·dŭ·rit) *adj.* stubborn and inflexible; hardhearted, not easily moved to pity. *I doubt he will change his mind; he is the most obdurate person I know.*

obfuscate (ob·'fus·kayt) *v.* 1. to make obscure or unclear, to muddle or make difficult to understand 2. to dim or darken. *Instead of clarifying the matter, Walter only obfuscated it further.*

obstreperous (ob·'strep·ĕ·rŭs) *adj.* noisily and stubbornly defiant; aggressively boisterous, unruly. *The obstreperous child refused to go to bed.*

obtrusive (ŏb·'troo·siv) *adj.* 1. prominent, undesirably noticeable 2. projecting, thrusting out 3. tending to push one's self or one's ideas upon others, forward, intrusive. *Thankfully, Minsun survived the accident, but she was left with several obtrusive scars.*

obtuse (ŏb·'toos) *adj.* 1. stupid and slow to understand 2. blunt, not sharp or pointed. *Please don't be so obtuse; you know what I mean.*

obviate ('ob·vi·ayt) *v.* to make unnecessary, get rid of. *Hiring Magdalena would obviate the need to hire a music tutor, for she is also a classical pianist.*

occult (ŏ·'kult) *adj.* 1. secret, hidden, concealed 2. involving the realm of the supernatural 3. beyond ordinary understanding, incomprehensible. *The rights and beliefs of the occult organization were finally made a matter of public record after a long investigation.*

odious ('oh·di·ŭs) *adj.* contemptible, hateful, detestable. *This is an odious policy that will only damage the environment more.*

officious (ŏ·'fish·ŭs) *adj.* meddlesome, bossy; eagerly offering unnecessary or unwanted advice. *My officious Aunt Midge is coming to the party, so be prepared for lots of questions and advice.*

oligarchy ('ol·ĭ·gahr·kee) *n.* form of government in which the power is in the hands of a select few. *The small governing body calls itself a democracy, but it is clearly an oligarchy.*

omnipotent (om·'nip·ŏ·tĕnt) *adj.* having unlimited or universal power or force. *In Greek mythology, Zeus was the most powerful god, but he was not omnipotent, since even his rule was often held in check by the unchangeable laws of the Three Fates.*

omniscient (om·'nish·ĕnt) *adj.* having infinite knowledge; knowing all things. *In a story with an omniscient narrator, we can hear the thoughts and feelings of all of the characters.*

onus ('oh·nŭs) *n.* duty or responsibility of doing something; task, burden. *It was Clark's idea, so the onus is on him to show us that it will work.*

opprobrious (ŏ·'proh·bri·ŭs) *adj.* 1. expressing contempt or reproach; scornful, abusive 2. bringing shame or disgrace. *It was inappropriate to make such opprobrious remarks in front of everybody.*

opulent (ˈop·yŭ·lĕnt) *adj.* 1. possessing great wealth, affluent 2. abundant, luxurious. *Lee is very wealthy, but he does not live an opulent lifestyle.*

ostensible (o·ˈsten·sĭ·bĕl) *adj.* seeming, appearing as such, put forward (as of a reason) but not necessarily so; pretended. *The ostensible reason for the meeting is to discuss the candidates, but I believe they have already made their decision.*

ostracize (ˈos·tră·sīz) *v.* to reject, cast out from a group or from society. *Kendall was ostracized after he repeatedly stole from his friends.*

overweening (ˈoh·vĕr·ˈwee·ning) *adj.* 1. presumptuously arrogant, overbearing 2. excessive, immoderate. *I quit because I couldn't stand to work for such an overweening boss.*

oxymoron (oks·i·ˈmoh·rŏn) *n.* a figure of speech containing a seemingly contradictory combination of expressions, such as *friendly fire*. *The term "non-working mother" is a contemptible oxymoron.*

palliate (ˈpal·i·ayt) *v.* 1. to make something less intense or severe, mitigate, alleviate; to gloss over, put a positive spin on 2. to provide relief from pain, relieve the symptoms of a disease or disorder. *The governor tried to palliate his malfeasance, but it soon became clear that he would not be able to prevent a scandal.*

pallor (ˈpal·ŏr) *n.* paleness, lack of color. *The fever subsided, but her pallor remained for several weeks.*

paradigm (ˈpār·ă·dīm) *n.* 1. something that serves as a model or example 2. set of assumptions, beliefs, values or practices that constitutes a way of understanding or doing things. *Elected "Employee of the Month," Winona is a paradigm of efficiency.*

pariah (pă·ˈrī·ă) *n.* an outcast, a rejected and despised person. *After he told a sexist joke, Jason was treated like a pariah by all of the women in the office.*

partisan (ˈpahr·ti·zăn) *n.* 1. a person fervently and often uncritically supporting a group or cause 2. a guerilla, a member of an organized body of fighters who attack or harass an enemy. *The partisan lobby could not see the logic of the opposing senator's argument and did not understand how the proposed legislation would infringe upon basic constitutional rights.*

paucity (ˈpaw·si·tee) *n.* scarcity, smallness of supply or quantity. *The paucity of food in the area drove the herd farther and farther to the south.*

peccadillo (pek·ă·ˈdil·oh) *n.* a trivial offense, a small sin or fault. *Don't make such a big deal out of a little peccadillo.*

pedantic (pi·ˈdăn·tik) *adj.* marked by a narrow, tiresome focus on or display of learning, especially of rules or trivial matters. *Her lessons were so pedantic that I found I was easily bored.*

pedestrian (pĕ·ˈdes·tri·ăn) *adj.* commonplace, trite; unremarkable, unimaginative, dull. *Although the film received critical acclaim, its pedestrian plot has been overused by screenwriters for decades.*

pellucid (pĕ·ˈloo·sid) *adj.* 1. translucent, able to be seen through with clarity 2. (e.g., of writing) very clear, easy to understand. *Senator Waterson's pellucid argument made me change my vote.*

penchant ('pen·chănt) *n.* a strong inclination or liking. *I have a real penchant for science fiction and spend hours reading my favorite authors every night.*

penultimate (pi·'nul·tĭ·mit) *adj.* next to last. *There's a real surprise for the audience in the penultimate scene.*

penury ('pen·yŭ·ree) *n.* extreme poverty, destitution. *After ten years of penury, it's good to be financially secure again.*

peremptory (pĕ·'remp·tŏ·ree) *adj.* 1. offensively self-assured, dictatorial 2. commanding, imperative, not allowing contradiction or refusal 3. putting an end to debate or action. *The father's peremptory tone ended the children's bickering.*

perfidious (pĕr·'fid·i·ŭs) *adj.* treacherous, dishonest; violating good faith, disloyal. *The perfidious knight betrayed his king.*

perfunctory (pĕr·'fungk·tŏ·ree) *adj.* done out of a sense of duty or routine but without much care or interest; superficial, not thorough. *We were not satisfied with his perfunctory work; we felt a more thorough job could have been done.*

perjury ('pur·jŭ·ree) *n.* the deliberate willful giving of false, misleading, or incomplete testimony while under oath. *William was convicted of perjury for lying about his whereabouts on the night of the crime.*

pernicious (pĕr·'nish·ŭs) *adj.* deadly, harmful, very destructive. *Nancy's opponent started a pernicious rumor that destroyed her chances of winning.*

personable ('pur·sŏ·nă·bĕl) *adj.* pleasing in appearance or manner, attractive. *Sandra is personable and well-liked by her peers.*

pertinacious (pur·tĭ·'nay·shŭs) *adj.* extremely stubborn or persistent; holding firmly to a belief, purpose, or course of action. *The pertinacious journalist finally uncovered the truth about the factory's illegal disposal of toxins.*

petrify ('pet·rĭ·fī) *v.* 1. to make hard or stiff like a stone 2. to stun or paralyze with fear, astonishment, or dread. *I was petrified when I heard the door open in the middle of the night.*

petulant ('pech·ŭ·lănt) *adj.* peevish; unreasonably or easily irritated or annoyed. *The pouting and sulking child could only be described as petulant!*

philistine ('fil·i·steen) *n.* a smug, ignorant person; someone who is uncultured and commonplace. *Richards thinks he is cosmopolitan, but he's really just a philistine.*

phoenix ('fee·niks) *n.* 1. a person or thing of unmatched beauty or excellence 2. a person or thing that has become renewed or restored after suffering calamity or apparent annihilation (after the mythological bird that periodically immolated itself and rose from the ashes as a new phoenix). *The phoenix is often used to symbolize something that is indomitable or immortal.*

pillage ('pil·ij) *v.* to forcibly rob of goods, especially in time of war; to plunder. *The barbarians pillaged the village before destroying it with fire.*

piquant ('pee·kănt) *adj.* 1. agreeably pungent, sharp or tart in taste 2. pleasantly stimulating or provocative. *The spicy shrimp salad is wonderfully piquant.*

pique (peek) *v.* to wound (someone's) pride, to offend; to arouse or provoke. *The article really piqued my interest in wildlife preservation.*

pith (pith) *n.* 1. the essential or central part; the heart or essence (of the matter, idea, experience, etc.) 2. (in biology) the soft, sponge-like central cylinder of the stems of most flowering plants. *Her brief, but concise, statement went right to the pith of the argument and covered the most important issues.*

placid ('plas·id) *adj.* calm and peaceful; free from disturbance or tumult. *Lake Placid is as calm and peaceful as its name suggests.*

plaintive ('playn·tiv) *adj.* expressing sorrow; mournful, melancholy. *Janice's plaintive voice made me decide to stay and comfort her longer.*

platitude ('plat·i·tood) *n.* a trite or banal statement, especially one uttered as if it were new. *Matthew offered me several platitudes but no real advice.*

plethora ('pleth·ŏ·ră) *n.* an overabundance, extreme excess. *There was a plethora of food at the reception.*

poignant ('poin·yănt) *adj.* 1. arousing emotion, deeply moving, touching 2. keenly distressing; piercing or incisive. *They captured the poignant reunion on film.*

polemical (pŏ·'lem·ik·ăl) *adj.* controversial, argumentative. *The analyst presented a highly polemical view of the economic situation.*

poseur (poh·'zur) *n.* someone who takes on airs to impress others; a phony. *My first impression of the arrogant newcomer told me that he was a poseur; I just had a hunch that he wasn't what he seemed to be.*

pragmatic (prag·'mat·ik) *adj.* practical, matter-of-fact; favoring utility. *Since we don't have money or time to waste, I think we should take the most pragmatic approach.*

precarious (pri·'kair·i·ŭs) *adj.* 1. fraught with danger 2. dangerously unsteady or insecure. *Steve, the "Crocodile Hunter," is constantly placing himself in very precarious positions.*

precept ('pree·sept) *n.* a rule establishing standards of conduct. *The headmaster reviewed the precepts of the school with the students.*

precipitous (pri·'sip·i·t ŭs) *adj.* 1. extremely steep, dropping sharply 2. hasty, rash, foolhardy. *Driving through the state park, we spotted a grizzly bear on a precipitous cliff and wondered if he would fall.*

pretentious (pri·'ten·shŭs) *adj.* showy, pompous, putting on airs. *Hannah thinks that being pretentious will make people like her, but she is sorely mistaken.*

prevaricate (pri·'var·ĭ·kayt) *v.* to tell lies, to stray from or evade the truth. *Quit prevaricating and tell me what really happened.*

primeval (prī·'mee·văl) *adj.* ancient, original, belonging to the earliest ages. *The primeval art found in the caves was discovered by accident.*

pristine ('pris·teen) *adj.* 1. in its original and unspoiled condition, unadulterated 2. clean, pure, free from contamination. *We were awed by the beauty of the pristine forest in northern Canada.*

prodigal ('prod·ĭ·găl) *adj.* 1. recklessly wasteful or extravagant, especially with money 2. given in great abundance, lavish or profuse. *The parable of the prodigal son shows what can happen when money is wasted.*

profligate ('prof·lĭ·git) *adj.* 1. recklessly wasteful or extravagant, prodigal 2. lacking moral restraint, dissolute. *The profligate man quickly depleted his fortune.*

proletariat (proh·lĕ·'tair·i·ăt) *n.* the working class, those who do manual labor to earn a living. *The proletariats demanded fewer hours and better wages.*

propinquity (proh·'ping·kwi·tee) *n.* 1. proximity, nearness 2. affinity, similarity in nature. *The two scientific elements demonstrate a remarkable propinquity.*

propitious (proh·'pish·ŭs) *adj.* auspicious, presenting favorable circumstances. *These are propitious omens indeed and foretell a good journey.*

prosaic (proh·'zay·ik) *adj.* unimaginative, ordinary, dull. *The prosaic novel was rejected by the publisher.*

proscribe (proh·'skrīb) *v.* 1. to prohibit, forbid; to banish or outlaw 2. to denounce or condemn. *The king proscribed the worship of idols in his kingdom.*

protean ('proh·tee·ăn) *adj.* taking many forms, changeable; variable, versatile. *In Native American mythology, the coyote is often called the "shape shifter" because he is such a protean character.*

protocol ('proh·tŏ·kawl) *n.* 1. etiquette, ceremony, or procedure with regard to people's rank or status 2. a first copy of a treaty or document. *Jackson was fired for repeatedly refusing to follow protocol.*

provident ('prov·i·dĕnt) *adj.* wisely providing for future needs; frugal, economical. *Because my parents were so provident, I didn't have to struggle to pay for college.*

proxy ('prok·see) *n.* 1. a person or agent authorized to represent or act for another 2. a document authorizing this substitution. *The president appointed a proxy to handle business matters during his absence.*

puerile ('pyoo·ĕ·rĭl) *adj.* 1. childish, immature 2. suitable only for children, belonging to or of childhood. *Andrew is a remarkably successful businessman for someone so puerile.*

pugnacious (pug·'nay·shŭs) *adj.* contentious, quarrelsome, eager to fight, belligerent. *Don't be so pugnacious—I don't want to fight.*

punctilious (pungk·'til·i·ŭs) *adj.* very conscientious and precise, paying great attention to details or trivialities, especially in regard to etiquette. *Kira is as punctilious in her personal affairs as she is in the workplace.*

pundit ('pun·dit) *n.* a learned person or scholar; one who is an authority on a subject. *The journalist consulted several legal pundits before drafting the article.*

pungent ('pun·jĕnt) *adj.* 1. having a strong, sharp taste or smell 2. penetrating, caustic, stinging. *I love the pungent taste of a good, strong curry.*

purloin (pŭr·'loin) *v.* to steal. *The thief purloined a sculpture worth thousands of dollars.*

purport ('pur·pohrt) *v.* 1. to be intended to seem, to have the appearance of being 2. propose or intend. *The letter purports to express your opinion on the matter.*

quaff (kwahf) *v.* to drink hurriedly or heartily; to swallow in large draughts. *He quickly quaffed three glasses of water.*

quail (kwayl) *v.* to draw back in fear, flinch, cower. *Mona quailed as soon as Otto entered the room.*

querulous ('kwer·ŭ·lŭs) *adj.* complaining, peevish, discontented. *He's a cantankerous and querulous old man, but I love him.*

queue (kyoo) *n.* 1. a line of people or vehicles waiting their turn 2. a pigtail. *Look how long the queue is! We'll be waiting for hours.*

quid pro quo (kwid proh 'kwoh) *n.* a thing given in return for something; an equal exchange or substitution. *Let's come up with a quid pro quo arrangement that will create a winning situation for both sides.*

quiescent (kwi·'es·ĕnt) *adj.* inactive, quiet, at rest; dormant, latent. *The volcano is quiescent at the moment, but who knows when it will erupt again.*

quintessence (kwin·'tes·ĕns) *n.* 1. the essence of a substance 2. the perfect example or embodiment of something. *Maura is the quintessence of kindness.*

quixotic (kwik·'sot·ik) *adj.* extravagantly chivalrous and unselfish; romantically idealistic, impractical. *His quixotic ways charmed all the women at the dance.*

quotidian (kwoh·'tid·i·ăn) *adj.* 1. daily 2. commonplace, pedestrian. *Prudence took her quotidian dose of medicine.*

rakish ('ray·kish) *adj.* 1. debonair, smartly dressed or mannered, jaunty in appearance or manner 2. unconventional and disreputable; dissolute or debauched. *The rakish young woman charmed everyone at the table.*

rancor ('rang·kŏr) *n.* a bitter feeling of ill will, long-lasting resentment. *Greg is full of rancor toward his brother, and this causes tension at family gatherings.*

rapacious (ră·'pay·shŭs) *adj.* excessively greedy and grasping (especially for money); voracious, plundering. *The rapacious general ordered his soldiers to pillage the town.*

raucous ('raw·kŭs) *adj.* 1. unpleasantly loud and harsh 2. boisterous, disorderly, disturbing the peace. *The raucous music kept us awake all night.*

reactionary (ree-ʹak·shŏ·ner·ee) *n.* a person who favors political conservativism; one who is opposed to progress or liberalism. *It should be an interesting marriage: he's a reactionary and she's as liberal as they come.*

recalcitrant (ri·ʹkal·si·trănt) *adj.* disobedient, unruly, refusing to obey authority. *The recalcitrant child was sent to the principal's office for the third time in a week.*

recidivism (ri·ʹsid·ĭ·vizm) *n.* a relapse or backslide, especially into antisocial or criminal behavior after conviction and punishment. *Allowing prisoners to earn their GEDs or college degrees has been shown to greatly reduce recidivism.*

recondite (ʹrek·ŏn·dīt) *adj.* 1. not easily understood, obscure, and abstruse 2. dealing with abstruse or profound matters. *He loves the challenge of grasping a recondite subject.*

refractory (ri·ʹfrak·tŏ·ree) *adj.* stubborn, unmanageable, resisting control or discipline. *Elena is a counselor for refractory children in an alternative school setting.*

regale (ri·ʹgayl) *v.* to delight or entertain with a splendid feast or pleasant amusement. *The king regaled his guests until the early morning hours.*

remonstrate (ri·ʹmon·strayt) *v.* 1. to say or plead in protest, objection, or opposition 2. to scold or reprove. *The children remonstrated loudly when their babysitter told them they couldn't watch that movie.*

renegade (ʹren·ĕ·gayd) *n.* 1. a deserter; one who rejects a cause, group, etc. 2. a person who rebels and becomes an outlaw. *The renegade soldier decided to join the guerilla fighters.*

renowned (ri·ʹnownd) *adj.* famous; widely known and esteemed. *The renowned historian Stephen Ambrose wrote many books that were popular with both scholars and the general public.*

repartee (rep·ăr·ʹtee) *n.* 1. a quick, witty reply 2. the ability to make witty replies. *He wasn't expecting such a sharp repartee from someone who was normally so quiet.*

replete (ri·ʹpleet) *adj.* 1. well-stocked or abundantly supplied 2. full, gorged. *The house was replete with expensive antiques.*

repose (ri·ʹpohz) *n.* 1. resting or being at rest 2. calmness, tranquility, peace of mind. *The wail of a police siren disturbed my repose.*

reprehensible (rep·ri·ʹhen·sĭ·běl) *adj.* deserving rebuke or censure. *The reprehensible behavior of the neighborhood bully angered everyone on the block.*

reprieve (ri·ʹpreev) *n.* 1. postponement or cancellation of punishment, especially of the death sentence 2. temporary relief from danger or discomfort. *The court granted him a reprieve at the last moment because of DNA evidence that absolved him.*

reprisal (ri·ʹprī·zăl) *n.* 1. an act of retaliation for an injury with the intent of inflicting at least as much harm in return 2. the practice of using political or military force without actually resorting to war. *The president promised a swift reprisal for the attack.*

reprobate ('rep·rŏ·bayt) *n.* an immoral or unprincipled person; one without scruples. *Edgar deemed himself a reprobate, a criminal, and a traitor in his written confession.*

repudiate (ri·'pyoo·di·ayt) *v.* to disown, disavow, reject completely. *Ms. Tallon has repeatedly repudiated your accusations.*

rescind (ri·'sind) *v.* to repeal or cancel; to void or annul. *They have rescinded their offer, so we must find another buyer.*

resonant ('rez·ŏ·nănt) *adj.* echoing, resounding. *The new announcer at the stadium has a wonderfully resonant voice.*

reticent ('ret·i·sĕnt) *adj.* tending to keep one's thoughts and feelings to oneself; reserved, untalkative, silent. *Annette is very reticent, so don't expect her to tell you much about herself.*

rigmarole ('rig·mă·rohl) (also *rigamarole*) *n.* 1. rambling, confusing, incoherent talk 2. a complicated, petty procedure. *We had to go through a great deal of rigmarole to get this approved.*

rogue (rohg) *n.* 1. a dishonest, unprincipled person 2. a pleasantly mischievous person 3. a vicious and solitary animal living apart from the herd. *Yesterday, that rogue hid all of my cooking utensils; today he's switched everything around in the cupboards!*

roil (roil) *v.* 1. to make a liquid cloudy or muddy 2. to stir up or agitate 3. to anger or annoy. *That you could even think such a thing really roils me.*

rubric ('roo·brik) *n.* 1. a class or category 2. a heading, title, or note of explanation or direction. *I would put this under the rubric of "quackery," not "alternative medicine."*

sacrilegious (sak·rĭ·'leej·ŭs) *adj.* disrespectful or irreverent toward something regarded as sacred. *Her book was criticized by the church for being sacrilegious.*

sagacious (să·'gay·shŭs) *adj.* having or showing sound judgment; perceptive, wise. *My sagacious uncle always gives me good, sound advice.*

salient ('say·li·ĕnt) *adj.* 1. conspicuous, prominent, highly noticeable; drawing attention through a striking quality 2. spring up or jutting out. *Jill's most salient feature is her stunning auburn hair.*

salutary ('sal·yŭ·ter·ee) *adj.* producing a beneficial or wholesome effect; remedial. *To promote better health, I've decided to move to a more salutary climate.*

sanctimonious (sangk·tĭ·'moh·nee·ŭs) *adj.* hypocritically pious or devout; excessively self-righteous. *The thief's sanctimonious remark that "a fool and his money are soon parted" only made the jury more eager to convict him.*

sangfroid (sahn·'frwah) *n.* composure, especially in dangerous or difficult circumstances. *I wish I had Jane's sangfroid when I find myself in a confrontational situation.*

sanguine ('sang·gwin) *adj.* 1. confidently cheerful, optimistic 2. of the color of blood; red. *People are drawn to her because of her sanguine and pleasant nature.*

sardonic (sahr·'don·ik) *adj.* sarcastic, mocking scornfully. *I was hurt by his sardonic reply.*

saturnine ('sat·ŭr·nīn) *adj.* gloomy, dark, sullen. *The saturnine child sulked for hours.*

savoir faire ('sav·wahr 'fair) *n.* knowledge of the right thing to do or say in a social situation; graceful tact. *Savoir faire is essential if you want to be a successful diplomat.*

schism ('siz·ĕm) *n.* a separation or division into factions because of a difference in belief or opinion. *The schism between the two parties was forgotten as they united around a common cause.*

scintilla (sin·'til·ă) *n.* a trace or particle; minute amount, iota. *She has not one scintilla of doubt about his guilt.*

scurvy ('skur·vee) *adj.* contemptible, mean. *That scurvy knave has ruined my plans again.*

sedulous ('sej·ŭ·lŭs) *adj.* diligent, persevering, hard working. *After years of sedulous research, the researchers discovered a cure.*

semantics (si·'man·tiks) *n.* 1. the study of meaning in language 2. the meaning, connotation, or interpretation of words, symbols, or other forms 3. the study of relationships between signs or symbols and their meanings. *He claims it's a matter of semantics, but the matter is not open to interpretation.*

sententious (sen·'ten·shŭs) *adj.* 1. expressing oneself tersely, pithy 2. full of maxims and proverbs offered in a self-righteous manner. *I was looking for your honest opinion, not a sententious reply.*

shiftless ('shift·lis) *adj.* lazy and inefficient; lacking ambition, initiative, or purpose. *My shiftless roommate has failed all of his classes.*

simian ('sim·i·ăn) *adj.* of or like an ape or monkey. *Creationists do not believe that humans have simian ancestors.*

sinuous ('sin·yoo·ŭs) *adj.* winding, undulating, serpentine. *It is dangerous to drive fast on such a sinuous road.*

slake (slayk) *v.* 1. to satisfy, quench 2. to reduce the intensity of, moderate, allay. *The deer slaked its thirst at the river.*

sodden ('sod·ĕn) *adj.* 1. thoroughly saturated, soaked 2. expressionless or dull, unimaginative. *Caught in an unexpected rainstorm, I was sodden by the time I reached the bus stop.*

solecism ('sol·ĕ·siz·ĕm) *n.* 1. a mistake in the use of language 2. violation of good manners or etiquette, impropriety. *Frank's solecism caused his debate team much embarrassment.*

sophistry ('sof·i·stree) *n.* clever but faulty reasoning; a plausible but invalid argument intended to deceive by appearing sound. *I was amused by his sophistry but knew he had a little more research to do before he presented his argument to the distinguished scholars in his field.*

sordid ('sor·did) *adj.* 1. dirty, wretched, squalid 2. morally degraded. *This sordid establishment should be shut down immediately.*

specious ('spee·shŭs) *adj.* 1. seemingly plausible but false 2. deceptively pleasing in appearance. *Vinnie did not fool me with his specious argument.*

spurious ('spyoor·i·ŭs) *adj.* false, counterfeit, not genuine or authentic. *The expert confirmed that the Willie Mays autograph was spurious.*

squalid ('skwol·id) *adj.* 1. filthy and wretched 2. morally repulsive, sordid. *The housing inspectors noted such deplorable and squalid living conditions in the building on Water Street that they were forced to evacuate the tenants.*

stoical ('stoh·i·kăl) *adj.* seemingly unaffected by pleasure or pain; indifferent, impassive. *He remained stoical while his wife told him she was leaving.*

stolid ('stol·id) *adj.* not feeling or showing emotion, impassive; not easily aroused or excited. *Maxine is a very stolid person, so it will be difficult to tell how she feels.*

stringent ('strin·jĕnt) *adj.* very strict, according to very rigorous rules, requirements or standards. *The stringent eligibility requirements greatly limited the number of candidates for the scholarship.*

stultify ('stul·tĭ·fī) *v.* 1. to impair or make ineffective, cripple 2. to make (someone) look foolish or incompetent. *Of course I'm angry! You stultified me at that meeting!*

stymie ('stī·mee) *v.* to hinder, obstruct, thwart; to prevent the accomplishment of something. *The negotiations were stymied by yet another attack.*

sublime (sŭ·'blīm) *adj.* having noble or majestic qualities; inspiring awe, adoration, or reverence; lofty, supreme. *Beethoven's music is simply sublime.*

subliminal (sub·'lim·ĭ·năl) *adj.* below the threshold of consciousness. *Subliminal advertising is devious but effective.*

subvert (sub·'vurt) *v.* 1. to overthrow 2. to ruin, destroy completely 3. to undermine. *She quietly subverted his authority by sharing internal information with outside agents.*

sundry ('sun·dree) *adj.* various, miscellaneous. *The sundry items in her backpack reveal a great deal about her personality.*

supercilious (soo·pĕr·'sil·i·ŭs) *adj.* haughty, scornful, disdainful. *Sunil's supercilious attitude and sarcastic remarks annoy me greatly.*

supplicant ('sup·lĭ·kănt) *n.* a person who asks humbly for something; one who beseeches or entreats. *The supplicants begged for forgiveness.*

surly ('sur·lee) *adj.* bad-tempered, gruff, or unfriendly in a way that suggests menace. *Emily received a surly greeting from the normally cheerful receptionist.*

surrogate ('sur·ŏ·git) *n.* a substitute; one who takes the place of another. *Martha agreed to be a surrogate mother for her sister.*

svelte (svelt) *adj.* slender and graceful, suave. *The svelte actress offered a toast to her guests.*

sycophant ('sik·ŏ·fănt) *n.* a person who tries to win the favor of influential or powerful people through flattery; a fawning parasite. *The president is surrounded by sycophants, so how will he really know if his ideas have merit?*

taciturn ('tas·i·turn) *adj.* habitually untalkative, reserved. *I've always known him to be taciturn, but yesterday he regaled me with tales of his hiking adventures.*

tangible ('tan·jĭ·bĕl) *adj.* able to be perceived by touch, palpable; real or concrete. *There is no tangible evidence of misconduct; it's all hearsay.*

tawdry ('taw·dree) *adj.* gaudy or showy but without any real value; flashy and tasteless. *I've never seen such a tawdry outfit as the three-tiered taffeta prom gown that the singer wore to the awards ceremony!*

teem (teem) *v.* to be full of; to be present in large numbers. *This city is teeming with tourists during the summer months.*

temerity (tĕ·'mer·i·tee) *n.* foolish disregard of danger; brashness, audacity. *This is no time for temerity; we must move cautiously to avoid any further damage.*

tenacious (tĕ·'nay·shŭs) *adj.* 1. holding firmly to something, such as a right or principle; persistent, stubbornly unyielding 2. holding firmly, cohesive 3. sticking firmly, adhesive 4. (of memory) retentive. *When it comes to fighting for equality, she is the most tenacious person I know.*

tendentious (ten·'den·shŭs) *adj.* biased, not impartial, partisan; supporting a particular cause or position. *The tendentious proposal caused an uproar on the Senate floor.*

tenet ('ten·it) *n.* a belief, opinion, doctrine or principle held to be true by a person, group, or organization. *This pamphlet describes the tenets of Amnesty International.*

tenuous ('ten·yoo·ŭs) *adj.* 1. unsubstantial, flimsy 2. having little substance or validity. *Though the connection between the two crimes seemed tenuous at first, a thorough investigation showed they were committed by the same person.*

timorous ('tim·ŏ·rŭs) *adj.* fearful, timid, afraid. *The stray dog was timorous, and it took a great deal of coaxing to get him to come near the car.*

toil (toil) *n.* exhausting labor or effort; difficult or laborious work. *v.* to work laboriously, labor strenuously. *Evan toiled for hours before solving the problem.*

totalitarian (toh·tal·i·'tair·i·ăn) *adj.* a form of government in which those in control neither recognize nor tolerate rival parties or loyalties, demanding total submission of the individual to the needs of the state. *The totalitarian regime fell quickly when the people revolted.*

tractable ('trak·tă·bĕl) *adj.* easily managed or controlled; obedient, docile. *In the novel* Brave New World, *the World Controllers use hypnosis and a "happiness drug" to make everyone tractable.*

transient ('tran·zhĕnt) *adj.* lasting only a very short time; fleeting, transitory, brief. *Their relationship was transient but profound.*

trenchant ('tren·chănt) *adj.* 1. penetrating, forceful, effective 2. extremely perceptive, incisive 3. clear-cut, sharply defined. *It was a trenchant argument, and it forced me to change my mind about the issue.*

tribunal (trī·'byoo·năl) *n.* a court of justice. *He will be sentenced for his war crimes by an international tribunal.*

truculent ('truk·yŭ·lĕnt) *adj.* 1. defiantly aggressive 2. fierce, violent 3. bitterly expressing opposition. *The outspoken council president gave a truculent speech arguing against the proposal.*

truncate ('trung·kayt) *v.* to shorten or terminate by (or as if by) cutting the top or end off. *The glitch in the software program truncated the lines of a very important document I was typing.*

tumultuous (too·'mul·choo· ŭs) *adj.* 1. creating an uproar, disorderly, noisy 2. a state of confusion, turbulence, or agitation, tumult. *It was another tumultuous day for the stock market, and fluctuating prices wreaked havoc for investors.*

turpitude ('tur·pi·tood) *n.* 1. wickedness 2. a corrupt or depraved act. *Such turpitude deserves the most severe punishment.*

umbrage ('um·brij) *n.* offense, resentment. *I took great umbrage at your suggestion that I twisted the truth.*

undulate ('un·jŭ·layt) *v.* to move in waves or in a wavelike fashion, fluctuate. *The curtains undulated in the breeze.*

untoward (un·'tohrd) *adj.* 1. contrary to one's best interest or welfare; inconvenient, troublesome, adverse 2. improper, unseemly, perverse. *Jackson's untoward remarks made Amelia very uncomfortable.*

upbraid (up·'brayd) *v.* to reprove, reproach sharply, condemn; admonish. *The child was upbraided for misbehaving during the ceremony.*

urbane (ur·'bayn) *adj.* elegant, highly refined in manners, extremely tactful and polite. *Christopher thinks he's so urbane, but he's really quite pedestrian.*

vacuous ('vak·yoo·ŭs) *adj.* empty, purposeless; senseless, stupid, inane. *This TV show is yet another vacuous sitcom.*

venal ('vee·năl) *adj.* easily bribed or corrupted; unprincipled. *The venal judge was removed and disbarred.*

venerable ('ven·ĕ·ră·bĕl) *adj.* worthy of reverence or respect because of age, dignity, character or position. *The venerable Jimmy Carter has just won the Nobel Peace Prize.*

verbose (vĕr·'bohs) *adj.* using more words than necessary; wordy, long-winded. *Her verbose letter rambled so much that it didn't seem to have a point.*

verisimilitude (ver·i·si·ˈmil·i·tood) *n.* the appearance of being true or real. *The movie aims for complete verisimilitude and has painstakingly recreated the details of everyday life in the 1920s.*

veritable (ˈver·i·tă·bĕl) *adj.* real, true, genuine. *Einstein was a veritable genius.*

vex (veks) *v.* 1. to annoy, irritate 2. to cause worry to. *I was completely vexed by his puerile behavior.*

vitriolic (vit·ri·ˈol·ik) *adj.* savagely hostile or bitter, caustic. *Her vitriolic attack on her opponent was so hostile that it may cost her the election.*

volatile (ˈvol·ă·til) *adj.* 1. varying widely, inconstant, changeable, fickle 2. unstable, explosive, likely to change suddenly or violently 3. (in chemistry) evaporating readily. *Dan's volatile personality has been compared to that of Dr. Jekyll and Mr. Hyde.*

voluble (ˈvol·yŭ·bĕl) *adj.* 1. talking a great deal and with great ease; language marked by great fluency; rapid, nimble speech 2. turning or rotating easily on an axis. *Your new spokesperson is very voluble and clearly comfortable speaking in front of large audiences.*

voracious (voh·ˈray·shŭs) *adj.* excessively greedy, rapacious; having a great appetite for something, devouring greedily. *I have always been a voracious reader and go through dozens of books every month.*

xenophobia (zen·ŏ·ˈfoh·bi·ă) *n.* a strong dislike, distrust, or fear of foreigners. *Many atrocities have been committed because of xenophobia.*

zenith (ˈzee·nith) *n.* 1. the highest point, top, peak 2. the point in the sky directly above the observer. *She is at the zenith of her career and has won every case this year.*

▶ PREFIXES, SUFFIXES, AND WORD ROOTS

A familiarity with common prefixes, suffixes, and word roots can dramatically improve your ability to determine the meaning of unfamiliar vocabulary words. The tables below list common prefixes, suffixes, and word roots; their meanings; an example of a word with that prefix, suffix, or word root; the meaning of that word; and a sentence that demonstrates the meaning of that word. Refer to this list often to refresh your memory and improve your vocabulary.

▶ PREFIXES

Prefixes are syllables added to the *beginnings* of words to change or add to their meaning. This table lists some of the most common prefixes in the English language. They are grouped together by similar meanings.

Prefix	Meaning	Example	Definition	Sentence
uni-	one	unify *v.*	to form into a single unit, to unite	The new leader was able to **unify** the three factions into one strong political party.
mono-	one	monologue *n.*	a long speech by one person or performer	I was very moved by the **monologue** in Scene III.
bi-	two	bisect *v.*	to divide into two equal parts	If you **bisect** a square, you will get two rectangles of equal size.
duo-	two	duality *n.*	having two sides or parts	The novel explores the **duality** of good and evil in humans.
tri-	three	triangle *n.*	a figure having three angles	In an isosceles **triangle**, two of the three angles are the same size.
quadri-	four	quadruped *n.*	an animal with four feet	Some **quadrupeds** evolved into bipeds.
tetra-	four	tetralogy *n.*	series of four related artistic works, such as plays, operas, novels, etc.	"Time Zone" was the fourth and final work in Classman's **tetralogy**.
quint-	five	quintuplets *n.*	five offspring born at one time	Each **quintuplet** weighed less than four pounds at birth.
pent-	five	pentameter *n.*	a line of verse (poetry) with five metrical feet	Most of Shakespeare's sonnets are written in iambic **pentameter**.
multi-	many	multifaceted *adj.*	having many sides	This is a **multifaceted** issue, and we must examine each side carefully.
poly-	many	polyglot *n.*	one who speaks or understands several languages	It's no wonder he's a **polyglot**; he's lived in eight different countries.
omni-	all	omniscient *adj.*	knowing all	Dr. Perez seems **omniscient**; she knows what all of us are thinking in class.
micro-	small	microcosm *n.*	little or miniature world; something representing something else on a very small scale	Some people say that Brooklyn Heights, the Brooklyn district across the river from the Wall Street area, is a **microcosm** of Manhattan.

Prefix	Meaning	Example	Definition	Sentence
mini-	small	minority *n.*	small group within a larger group	John voted for Bridget, but he was in the **minority**; most people voted for Elaine.
macro-	large	macrocosm *n.*	the large scale world or universe; any great whole	Any change to the microcosm will eventually affect the **macrocosm**.
ante-	before	anticipate *v.*	to give advance thought to; foresee; expect	His decades of experience enabled him to **anticipate** the problem.
pre-	before	precede *v.*	to come before in time or order	The appetizers **preceded** the main course.
post-	after	postscript *n.*	message added after the close of a letter	His **postscript** was almost as long as his letter!
inter-	between	intervene *v.*	to come between	Romeo, trying to make peace, **intervened** in the fight between Tybalt and Mercutio.
inter-	together	interact *v.*	to act upon or influence each other	The psychologist took notes as she watched the children **interact**.
intra-	within	intravenous *adj.*	within or into a vein	She could not eat and had to be fed **intravenously** for three days.
intro-	into, within	introvert *n.*	a person whose attention is largely directed inward, toward himself or herself; a shy or withdrawn person	Unlike his flamboyant sister, quiet Zeke was a real **introvert**.
in-	in, into	induct *v.*	to bring in (to a group)	She was **inducted** into the honor society.
ex-	out, from	expel *v.*	to drive out or away	Let's **expel** the invaders!
circum-	around	circumscribe *v.*	to draw a line around; to mark the limits of	She carefully **circumscribed** the space that would become her office.
sub-	under	subvert *v.*	to bring about the destruction of, overthrow; to undermine	His attempt to **subvert** my authority will cost him his job.
super-	above, over	supervisor *n.*	one who watches over	Alex accepted the promotion to **supervisor** and was comfortable with the duties and responsibilities of the office.
con-	with, together	consensus *n.*	general agreement	After hours of debate, the group finally reached a **consensus** and selected a candidate.

Prefix	Meaning	Example	Definition	Sentence
non-	not	nonviable *adj.*	not able to live or survive	The farmer explained that the seedling was **nonviable.**
in-	not	invariable *adj.*	not changing	The weather here is **invariable**— always sunny and warm.
un-	not, against	unmindful *adj.*	not conscious or aware of; forgetful	For better or worse, he is **unmindful** of office politics.
contra-	against	contradict *v.*	to state that (what is said) is untrue; to state the opposite of	I know we don't have to agree on everything, but she **contradicts** *everything* I say.
anti-	against, opposite	antipode *n.*	exact or direct opposite	North is the **antipode** of south.
counter-	against, opposing	counter-productive *adj.*	working against production	Complaining is **counterproductive**.
dis-	away	dispel *v.*	to drive away	To **dispel** rumors that I was quitting, I scheduled a series of meetings for the next three months.
dis-	not, opposite of	disorderly *adj.*	not having order; messy, untidy, uncontrolled or unruly	Two people were hurt when the crowd became **disorderly** during the protest.
mis-	wrong, ill	misuse *v.*	to use wrongly	She **misused** her authority when she reassigned Charlie to a new team.
mal-	bad, wrong	maltreat *v.*	to treat badly or wrongly	After the dog saved his life, he swore he would never **maltreat** another animal.
mal-	ill	malaise *n.*	feeling of discomfort or illness	The **malaise** many women feel during the first few months of pregnancy is called "morning sickness."
pseudo-	false, fake	pseudonym *n.*	false or fake name	Mark Twain is a **pseudonym** for Samuel Clemens.
auto-	by oneself or by itself	automaton *n.*	a robot; a person who seems to act mechanically and without thinking	The workers on the assembly line looked like **automatons**.
co-	together with; jointly	cohesive *adj.*	having a tendency to bond or stick together; united	Though they came from different backgrounds, they have formed a remarkably **cohesive** team.

▶ **SUFFIXES**

Suffixes are syllables added to the *ends* of words to change or add to their meaning. This table lists some of the most common suffixes in the English language. They are grouped together by similar meanings.

Suffix	Meaning	Example	Definition	Sentence
-en	to cause to become	broaden *v.*	to make more broad, widen	Traveling around the world will **broaden** your understanding of other cultures.
-ate	to cause to be	resuscitate *v.*	to bring or come back to life or consciousness; to revive	Thanks to a generous gift from an alumnus, we were able to **resuscitate** the study-abroad program.
-ify/-fy	to make or cause to be	electrify *v.*	to charge with electricity	The singer **electrified** the audience with her performance.
-ize	to make, to give	alphabetize *v.*	to put in alphabetical order	Please **alphabetize** these files for me.
-al	capable of, suitable for	practical *adj.*	suitable for use; involving activity, as distinct from study or theory	He has years of **practical**, on-the-job experience.
-ial	pertaining to	commercial *adj.*	of or engaged in commerce	**Commercial** vehicles must have special license plates.
-ic	pertaining to	aristocratic *adj.*	of or pertaining to the aristocracy	Though he was never rich or powerful, he has very **aristocratic** manners.
-ly	resembling, having the qualities of	tenderly *adv.*	done with tenderness; gently, delicately, lovingly	He held the newborn baby **tenderly** in his arms.
-ly	in the manner of	boldly *adv.*	in a bold manner	Despite his fear, he stepped **boldly** onto the stage.
-ful	full of	meaningful *adj.*	significant, full of meaning	When Robert walked into the room with Annette, she cast me a **meaningful** glance.
-ous/-ose	full of	humorous *adj.*	full of humor, funny	His **humorous** speech made the evening go by quickly.
-ive	having the quality of	descriptive *adj.*	giving a description	The letter was so **descriptive** that I could picture every place he had been.
-less	lacking, free of	painless *adj.*	without pain, not causing pain	The doctor assured me that it is a **painless** procedure.
-ish	having the quality of	childish *adj.*	like a child; unsuitable for a grown person	He didn't get the job because of his **childish** behavior during the interview.

Suffix	Meaning	Example	Definition	Sentence
-ance/ -ence	quality or state of	tolerance *n.*	willingness or ability to tolerate a person or thing	He has a high level of **tolerance** for rudeness.
-acy	quality or state of	indeterminacy *n.*	state or quality of being undetermined (without defined limits) or vague	The **indeterminacy** of his statement made it impossible to tell which side he favored.
-tion	act, state or condition of	completion *n.*	the act of completing; the state of being completed or finished	The second siren signaled the **completion** of the fire drill.
-or/-er	one who does or performs the action of	narrator *n.*	one who tells the story, gives an account of	A first-person **narrator** is usually not objective.
-atrium/ -orium	place for	arboretum *n.*	a garden devoted primarily to trees and shrubs	They built a deck with an **arboretum** for their bonsai tree collection.
-ary	place for, pertaining to	sanctuary *n.*	a sacred place, a refuge	With three noisy roommates, Ellen frequently sought the quiet **sanctuary** of the library.
-cide	kill	pesticide *n.*	substance for killing insects	This **pesticide** is also dangerous for humans.
-ism	quality, state or condition of; doctrine of	optimism *n.*	belief that things will turn out for the best; tendency to take a hopeful view of things	Her **optimism** makes people want to be around her.
-ity	quality or state of	morality *n.*	state or quality of being moral	He argued that the basic **morality** of civilized societies hasn't changed much over the centuries.
-itis	inflammation of	tonsillitis *n.*	inflammation and infection of the tonsils	Her **tonsillitis** was so severe that doctors had to remove her tonsils immediately.
-ment	act or condition of	judgment *n.*	ability to judge or make decisions wisely; act of judging	He exercised good **judgment** by keeping his mouth shut during the meeting.
-ology	the study of	zoology *n.*	the scientific study of animal life	She took a summer job at the zoo because of her strong interest in **zoology**.

▶ COMMON LATIN WORD ROOTS

Many words in the English language have their origins in Latin. The table below shows the original Latin words that we have used to create various English words. The Latin words serve as *roots*, providing the core meaning of the words; prefixes, suffixes, and other alterations give each word its distinct meaning. The word roots are listed in alphabetical order.

Root	Meaning	Example	Definition	Sentence
amare	to love	amorous *adj.*	readily showing or feeling love	She told him to stop his **amorous** advances as she was already engaged.
audire	to hear	audience *n.*	assembled group of listeners or spectators; people within hearing	The **audience** was stunned when the game show host slapped the contestant.
bellum	war	belligerent *adj.*	inclined to fight; hostile, aggressive	The citizens feared that their **belligerent** leader would start an unjust war.
capere	to take	captivate *v.*	to capture the fancy of	The story **captivated** me from the beginning; I couldn't put the book down.
dicere	to say, speak	dictate *v.*	to state or order; to say what needs to be written down	She began to **dictate** her notes into the microphone.
duco	to lead	conduct *v.*	to lead or guide (thorough)	He **conducted** a detailed tour of the building.
equus	equal	equilibrium *n.*	a state of balance	I have finally achieved an **equilibrium** between work and leisure.
facere	to make or do	manufacture *v.*	to make or produce	The clothes are **manufactured** here in this factory.
lucere	to light	lucid *adj.*	very clear	No one could possibly have misunderstood such a **lucid** explanation.
manus	hand	manicure *n.*	cosmetic treatment of the fingernails	To maintain her long fingernails, she gets a **manicure** every week.
medius	middle	median *n., adj.*	middle point; middle in a set of numbers	The **median** household income in this wealthy neighborhood is $89,000.
mittere	to send	transmit *v.*	to send across	The message was **transmitted** over the intercom.

Root	Meaning	Example	Definition	Sentence
omnis	all, every	omnipresent *adj.*	present everywhere	That top-40 song is **omnipresent**; everywhere I go, I hear it playing.
plicare	to fold	application *n.*	putting one thing on another; making a formal request	His loan **application** was denied because of his poor credit history.
ponere/ positum	to place	position *n.*	the place a person or thing occupies	Although he is only 22, he holds a very powerful **position** in the company.
protare	to carry	transport *v.*	to carry across	The goods will be **transported** by boat.
quarere	to ask, question	inquiry *n.*	act of inquiry, investigation, or questioning	The **inquiry** lasted several months but yielded no new information.
scribere	to write	scribe *n.*	person who makes copies of writings	The **scribe** had developed thick calluses on his fingers from years of writing.
sentire	to feel	sentient *adj.*	capable of feeling	No **sentient** beings should be used for medical research.
specere	to look at	spectacle *n.*	striking or impressive sight	The debate was quite a **spectacle;** you should have seen the candidates attack one another.
spirare	to breathe	respiration *n.*	the act of breathing	His **respiration** was steady, but he remained unconscious.
tendere	to stretch	extend *v.*	to make longer, stretch out	Please **extend** the deadline by two weeks so we can complete the project properly.
verbum	word	verbatim *adj., adv.*	word for word	The student failed because she had copied an article **verbatim** instead of writing her own essay.

▶ COMMON GREEK WORD ROOTS

Many other English words have their origins in the ancient Greek language. The table below shows the Greek words that we have used to create various English words. The Greek words serve as **roots,** providing the core meaning of the words; prefixes, suffixes, and other alterations give each word its distinct meaning. The word roots are listed in alphabetical order.

Root	Meaning	Example	Definition	Sentence
bios	life	biology *n.*	the science of living organisms	He is majoring in **biology** and plans to go to medical school.
chronos	time	chronological *adj.*	arranged in the order in which things occurred	The story is confusing because she did not put the events in **chronological** order.
derma	skin	dermatology *n.*	branch of medical science dealing with the skin and its diseases	She has decided to study **dermatology** because she has always been plagued by rashes.
gamos	marriage, union	polygamy *n.*	the practice or custom of having more than one spouse or mate at a time	Throughout history, certain cultures have practiced **polygamy,** but it is uncommon today.
genos	race, sex, kind	genocide *n.*	the deliberate extermination of one race of people	The recent **genocide** in Bosnia has created a crisis in orphaned children.
geo	earth	geography *n.*	the study of the Earth's surface; the surface or topographical features of a place	The **geography** of this region made it difficult for the different tribes to interact.
graphein	to write	calligraphy *n.*	beautiful or elegant handwriting	She used **calligraphy** when she addressed the wedding invitations.
krates	member of a group	democrat *n.*	one who believes in or advocates democracy as a principle of government	I have always been a **democrat,** but I refuse to join the Democratic Party.
kryptos	hidden, secret	cryptic *adj.*	concealing meaning, puzzling	He left such a **cryptic** message on my answering machine that I don't know what he wanted.
metron	to measure	metronome *n.*	device with a pendulum that beats at a determined rate to measure time/rhythm	She used a **metronome** to help her keep the proper pace as she played the song.

Root	Meaning	Example	Definition	Sentence
morphe	form	polymorphous *adj.*	having many forms	Most mythologies have a **polymorphous** figure, a "shape shifter" who can be both animal and human.
pathos	suffering, feeling	pathetic *adj.*	arousing feelings of pity or sadness	Willy Loman is a complex character who is both **pathetic** and heroic.
philos	loving	xenophile *n.*	a person who is attracted to foreign peoples, cultures, or customs	Alex is a **xenophile**; I doubt he will ever come back to the States.
phobos	fear	xenophobe *n.*	person who fears or hates foreigners or strange cultures or customs	Don't expect Len to go on the trip; he's a **xenophobe**.
photos	light	photobiotic *adj.*	living or thriving only in the presence of light	Plants are **photobiotic** and will die without light.
podos	foot	podiatrist *n.*	an expert in diagnosis and treatment of ailments of the human foot	The **podiatrist** saw that the ingrown toenail had become infected.
pseudein	to deceive	pseudonym *n.*	false name	George Eliot is a **pseudonym** for Mary Ann Evans.
pyr	fire	pyromaniac *n.*	one who has a compulsion to set things on fire	The warehouse fire was not an accident; it was set by a **pyromaniac**.
soma	body	psychosomatic *adj.*	of or involving both the mind and body	In a **psychosomatic** illness, physical symptoms are caused by emotional distress.
tele	distant	telescope *n.*	optical instrument for making distant objects appear larger and nearer when viewed through the lens	While Galileo did not invent the **telescope**, he was the first to use it to study the planets and stars.
therme	heat	thermos *n.*	insulated jug or bottle that keeps liquids hot or cold	The **thermos** kept my coffee hot all afternoon.

3

Vocabulary in Context

The vocabulary section of a Civil Service test often includes a section of vocabulary in context questions. For this part of the test, you will be asked to identify the meaning of vocabulary words used in sentences. Since you will not be able to use a dictionary during the test, it is important to develop vocabulary strategies that will boost your score and give you the advantage you need.

As you might expect, vocabulary in context questions ask you to determine the meanings of particular words. To prepare for this section of the test, recall the skills you developed at an early age. First, it is a good idea to be an active reader. This is a skill you can practice every day. As you read the daily newspaper, your favorite magazine, or a good book, have a dictionary handy. Look up as many unfamiliar words as you can so that your bank of vocabulary words becomes as large as possible. Second, be aware that you can use the context of a sentence to help you detect the meaning of a word. Simply put, this means that you can look for clues in and around the vocabulary word. For practice, try the following exercise to see how this can be done.

▶ FINDING MEANING FROM CONTEXT

As a result of many meetings held by the Human Resources Department, a memo was written to help hiring supervisors present information about new procedures that benefit company, staff, and new employees during a new employee orientation seminar. The new procedures create a win-win situation for all concerned, and the Human Resources Department wants to make sure that those people who are instrumental in making the program work have all the information they need. Imagine that your title is Hiring Supervisor, and you receive the following memorandum from the Human Resources department. Read it carefully. Circle any words that are unfamiliar to you, but do not use a dictionary to look them up just yet.

TO: Hiring Supervisors
FROM: Human Resources
RE: New Employees

In order to acquaint new employees with office practices and procedures, the *New Employee's Introduction Manual* has been compiled. This manual should be distributed to all new hires during an orientation seminar that you will conduct one week before a new employee begins work. During orientation, be sure to point out that not only does the information in the manual inform new employees about office protocol and employee benefits, but it gives them a sense of the new family they are about to join. As you leaf through the manual with new hires, note that the manual begins with basic office etiquette, procedures, and dress codes and then there is a segue to important information about pay schedules and benefits. Explain to your orientation group that with this manual in hand, new employees will have a more global view of the company. They will know what to expect and can ask questions that will make their new position a little more comfortable on the first day. The benefits of the orientation seminar, in addition to the manual, will make our workplace a more cohesive and productive environment for all employees.

As you read, you may have circled *protocol* or *segue*. By looking for context clues—the way the words are used in the paragraph—you can figure out what these words mean.

What does *protocol* mean?

Reread the sentence with the word *protocol*.

During orientation, be sure to point out that not only does the information in the manual inform new employees about office *protocol* and employee benefits, but it gives them a sense of the new family they are about to join.

Even if you have no idea what *protocol* means, you can still tell something about the word by how it is used—by examining the words and ideas surrounding it. This is called determining word meaning through context. Like detectives looking for clues at a crime scene, you must look at the passage for clues that will uncover the definition of the word.

Given the sentence you have here, you can begin to consider the definition of *protocol*. Since the manual informs new employees about office protocol and employee benefits, this tells you that protocol must be a procedure or system designed to make things run smoothly in the office. As you read the next sentence in the memo, you see that the sections of the manual cover many aspects: etiquette, procedures, dress codes, salaries, and employee benefits. At this point, you should be able to take a pretty good guess at the definition of the word *protocol*.

1. The best definition of the word *protocol* is
   a. a meeting's agenda.
   b. a code of correct procedure.
   c. a salary schedule.

Choice **a** cannot be correct, because nowhere in the passage does it state that protocol is a list of items covered in a meeting. While a salary schedule, choice **c**, is determined by a certain procedure, it is only part of the scope of an office system. The correct answer is choice **b**, a code of correct procedure.

What does *segue* mean?
Look again at the sentence in which *segue* is used.

As you leaf through the manual with new hires, note that the manual begins with basic office etiquette, procedures, and dress codes and then there is a *segue* to important information about pay schedules and benefits.

Again, even if you have no idea what *segue* means, you can still tell what kind of word it is by the way it is used in the sentence.

2. Since the word *segue* falls between a list of basic office etiquette, procedure, and dress code *and* important information about pay schedules and benefits, you know this word is a word of
   a. interference in the sentence.
   b. transition in the sentence.

Choice **b** is correct; *segue* signifies a transition. There is one context clue. As the hiring supervisor leafs through the manual, he or she pages through all sections of the text, highlighting the basic elements contained in the opening chapters and then notes that the chapters switch or move to important facts about salaries and benefits.

3. *Segue*, in this case, can be defined as information that is
   a. a disorganized flow of ideas.
   b. merely sketchy details and descriptions.
   c. uninterrupted movement from one stage to the next.
   d. wordy and verbose language.

The correct answer is choice **c**, uninterrupted movement from one state to the next. It cannot be choice **b** or **d** because there is no indication that anything in the manual is omitted or for that matter, wordy or verbose. Choice **a** is not a suitable answer because the manual, as it is outlined, appears to be well-ordered.

How Much Context Do You Need?

In the previous example, you would still be able to understand the main message of the memorandum even if you did not know—or could not figure out—the meanings of *protocol* and *segue*. In some cases, though, your understanding of a sentence depends on your understanding of a particular word or phrase. For example, can you understand the following sentence without knowing what *adversely* means?

The new policy will *adversely* affect all employees.

You might not understand it in this short sentence, and if you are an employee, you certainly would want to know how you are going to be affected. More defining clues for the word *adversely* will help you know whether it is something good or bad.

The new policy will *adversely* affect all employees; it will freeze their pay, limit their vacation time, and reduce their health benefits.

4. In the sentence, *adversely* most nearly means
   a. mildly or slightly.
   b. regularly or steadily.
   c. negatively or unfavorably.
   d. immediately or swiftly.

The correct answer is choice **c**, negatively or unfavorably. The addition of the second part of the sentence now tells you exactly how the new policy will affect the employees: "It will freeze their pay, limit their vacations, and reduce their benefits." It certainly is not choice **a**, a slight or mild change, nor is it choice **b**, a regular or steady change. You do not know if it is an immediate or swift change, choice **d**, because the sentence says nothing about the time frame in which this change will take place. Remember, good detectives do not make assumptions they are not able to support with facts, and there are no facts in this sentence to support the assumption that the changes will take place immediately. Thus, choice **c** is the best answer.

You may also have noticed that *adversely* is very similar to the word *adversary*. If you know that an *adversary* is a hostile opponent or enemy, then you know that *adversely* is not likely to be something positive. Or, if you know the word *adversity*—hardship or misfortune—then you know that *adversely* must mean something negative or difficult. All of these words share the same root: *advers-*. The only change is in the endings.

Being able to determine the meaning of unfamiliar words from their context is an essential vocabulary skill. Sometimes you will encounter unfamiliar words whose meaning is indecipherable without a dictionary. More often than not, though, a careful look at the context will give you enough clues to interpret the definitions.

PRACTICE QUESTIONS

Choose the best vocabulary word to fill the blank. Use this answer grid to fill in your answers to the questions.

1.	ⓐ	ⓑ	ⓒ	ⓓ	26.	ⓐ	ⓑ	ⓒ	ⓓ
2.	ⓐ	ⓑ	ⓒ	ⓓ	27.	ⓐ	ⓑ	ⓒ	ⓓ
3.	ⓐ	ⓑ	ⓒ	ⓓ	28.	ⓐ	ⓑ	ⓒ	ⓓ
4.	ⓐ	ⓑ	ⓒ	ⓓ	29.	ⓐ	ⓑ	ⓒ	ⓓ
5.	ⓐ	ⓑ	ⓒ	ⓓ	30.	ⓐ	ⓑ	ⓒ	ⓓ
6.	ⓐ	ⓑ	ⓒ	ⓓ	31.	ⓐ	ⓑ	ⓒ	ⓓ
7.	ⓐ	ⓑ	ⓒ	ⓓ	32.	ⓐ	ⓑ	ⓒ	ⓓ
8.	ⓐ	ⓑ	ⓒ	ⓓ	33.	ⓐ	ⓑ	ⓒ	ⓓ
9.	ⓐ	ⓑ	ⓒ	ⓓ	34.	ⓐ	ⓑ	ⓒ	ⓓ
10.	ⓐ	ⓑ	ⓒ	ⓓ	35.	ⓐ	ⓑ	ⓒ	ⓓ
11.	ⓐ	ⓑ	ⓒ	ⓓ	36.	ⓐ	ⓑ	ⓒ	ⓓ
12.	ⓐ	ⓑ	ⓒ	ⓓ	37.	ⓐ	ⓑ	ⓒ	ⓓ
13.	ⓐ	ⓑ	ⓒ	ⓓ	38.	ⓐ	ⓑ	ⓒ	ⓓ
14.	ⓐ	ⓑ	ⓒ	ⓓ	39.	ⓐ	ⓑ	ⓒ	ⓓ
15.	ⓐ	ⓑ	ⓒ	ⓓ	40.	ⓐ	ⓑ	ⓒ	ⓓ
16.	ⓐ	ⓑ	ⓒ	ⓓ	41.	ⓐ	ⓑ	ⓒ	ⓓ
17.	ⓐ	ⓑ	ⓒ	ⓓ	42.	ⓐ	ⓑ	ⓒ	ⓓ
18.	ⓐ	ⓑ	ⓒ	ⓓ	43.	ⓐ	ⓑ	ⓒ	ⓓ
19.	ⓐ	ⓑ	ⓒ	ⓓ	44.	ⓐ	ⓑ	ⓒ	ⓓ
20.	ⓐ	ⓑ	ⓒ	ⓓ	45.	ⓐ	ⓑ	ⓒ	ⓓ
21.	ⓐ	ⓑ	ⓒ	ⓓ	46.	ⓐ	ⓑ	ⓒ	ⓓ
22.	ⓐ	ⓑ	ⓒ	ⓓ	47.	ⓐ	ⓑ	ⓒ	ⓓ
23.	ⓐ	ⓑ	ⓒ	ⓓ	48.	ⓐ	ⓑ	ⓒ	ⓓ
24.	ⓐ	ⓑ	ⓒ	ⓓ	49.	ⓐ	ⓑ	ⓒ	ⓓ
25.	ⓐ	ⓑ	ⓒ	ⓓ	50.	ⓐ	ⓑ	ⓒ	ⓓ

1. The _____ union president differs from the past union president on employee reform issues.
   a. talkative
   b. accomplished
   c. artificial
   d. incumbent

2. The _____ data supports the belief that there has been an increase in population in the county.
   a. nominal
   b. demographic
   c. practical
   d. nocturnal

3. The _____ collected from real estate taxes helped to balance the town budget.
   a. domain
   b. remainder
   c. revenue
   d. assessment

4. She pretended to be _____ about the new job opportunity, but secretly she was very excited.
   a. dedicated
   b. receptive
   c. candid
   d. blasé

5. We were tired when we reached the _____, but the spectacular view of the valley below was worth the hike.
   a. circumference
   b. summit
   c. fulcrum
   d. nadir

6. The suit had a/an _____ odor, as if it had been stored in a trunk for a long time.
   a. aged
   b. scented
   c. musty
   d. decrepit

7. Since his workplace was so busy and noisy, he longed most of all for _____.
   a. solitude
   b. association
   c. loneliness
   d. irrelevancy

8. The teacher put the crayons on the bottom shelf to make them _____ to the young children.
   a. accessible
   b. receptive
   c. eloquent
   d. ambiguous

9. My computer was state-of-the-art when I bought it three years ago, but now it is _____.
   a. current
   b. dedicated
   c. unnecessary
   d. outmoded

10. Visiting all the coffee shops in the city, they were on a _____ to find the perfect cup of coffee.
   a. surge
   b. quest
   c. discovery
   d. cadence

11. George developed an _____ plan to earn the extra money he needed to start his own business.
   a. elitist
   b. irrational
   c. aloof
   d. ingenious

12. We knew everything about the newest member of our group; she was very _____.
   a. expressive
   b. secretive
   c. reserved
   d. artistic

13. I have always liked your positive attitude; it has _____ affected our working relationship.
   a. adversely
   b. shamelessly
   c. candidly
   d. favorably

14. Dog-sitting for Buddy is easy to do; he is a _____ and obedient pet.
   a. delectable
   b. commonplace
   c. meddlesome
   d. docile

15. The directions to the new office were _____, and I had no trouble finding it in time for work.
   a. priceless
   b. arduous
   c. explicit
   d. embodied

16. If your drinking water is not _____, it could cause serious health problems.
   a. valid
   b. quenchable
   c. impure
   d. potable

17. The new board member said she would vote in favor of the proposed city ordinance because it _____ many of the points discussed earlier this year.
   a. encompassed
   b. released
   c. reminisced
   d. dispersed

18. Rachel _____ a plan to become a millionaire by age thirty.
   a. conformed
   b. devised
   c. decreased
   d. condoned

19. Wanting to make a good impression, he found himself in a _____ about the right tie to wear to the business meeting.
   a. prestige
   b. redundancy
   c. quandary
   d. deficit

20. Since Mark needed to pass the exam, he made studying a _____ over watching his favorite television show.
   a. priority
   b. conformity
   c. perplexity
   d. concept

21. Hoping to win a prize for the best costume, Mark dressed _____ in bright red suspenders and a purple tie.
   a. eminently
   b. virtuously
   c. conspicuously
   d. obscurely

22. Brad fell asleep during the movie because it had a very _____ plot.
   a. monotonous
   b. torrid
   c. ample
   d. vital

23. To get the promotion she wanted, she _____ that it was best to go back to school to get her master's degree as soon as she could.
   a. supposed
   b. surmised
   c. presumed
   d. resolved

24. The narrator's description was an accurate _____ of a true southern family.
   a. portrayal
   b. council
   c. disguise
   d. reunion

25. Due to slippery road conditions and the slope of the narrow, winding highway, the car _____ down the steep mountainous road.
   a. dissented
   b. ventilated
   c. careened
   d. agitated

26. The fire alarm _____ beckoned the volunteer firefighters of the small community to come to action.
   a. approvingly
   b. significantly
   c. symbolically
   d. audibly

27. After running an early 5K race, Simone _____ devoured a hearty breakfast.
   a. dynamically
   b. voraciously
   c. generously
   d. beneficially

28. The car rental company considered the scratches on the driver's door to be caused by a minor _____.
   a. mishap
   b. attraction
   c. reflex
   d. duplicate

29. The participants in the road rally agreed to _____ near the village commons at five o'clock.
   a. rendezvous
   b. scatter
   c. filibuster
   d. disperse

30. Understanding the world economic conditions, the recent graduates spoke _____ about job prospects for the future.
   a. warily
   b. luxuriously
   c. measurably
   d. narrowly

31. Being a direct relative of the deceased, her claim to the estate was _____.
   a. optional
   b. vicious
   c. prominent
   d. legitimate

32. The hail _____ the cornfield until the entire crop was lost.
   a. belittled
   b. pummeled
   c. rebuked
   d. commended

33. The Earth Day committee leader placed large garbage bins in the park to _____ Saturday's cleanup.
   a. confound
   b. pacify
   c. integrate
   d. facilitate

34. Her rapport with everyone in the office _____ the kind of interpersonal skills that all of the employees appreciated.
  a. prevailed
  b. diverged
  c. exemplified
  d. varied

35. The _____ of the two rivers provided the perfect place to build a new state park.
  a. assumption
  b. confluence
  c. seclusion
  d. treatise

36. The abundant mutual fund research information on the website was _____ with tips for new investors.
  a. inflated
  b. replete
  c. constricted
  d. embellished

37. The intricate and _____ language of the contract needed to be interpreted by an attorney.
  a. essential
  b. fundamental
  c. convoluted
  d. straightforward

38. Do you have the _____ paperwork you need to register for the class?
  a. punitive
  b. grandiose
  c. restorative
  d. requisite

39. Do not _____ yourself; you must pass the last exam of the semester to graduate.
  a. delude
  b. depreciate
  c. relinquish
  d. prohibit

40. When you address the members of the committee, be sure to give a _____ description of the new office procedures.
  a. principled
  b. determined
  c. comprehensive
  d. massive

41. Although Hunter was _____ to reveal information to us when we first met him, he soon began to talk more than anyone.
   a. customary
   b. reticent
   c. animated
   d. voluntary

42. The darkening skies in the west were a _____ to the dangerous thunderstorm that summer afternoon.
   a. tedium
   b. precursor
   c. preference
   d. momentum

43. The news was no longer secret; Martin Kemp _____ told the press that he had accepted the nomination as board chairperson.
   a. repulsively
   b. reputedly
   c. perpetually
   d. principally

44. After an hour of heavy rain, the thunderstorm _____, and we were able to continue our golf game.
   a. abated
   b. germinated
   c. constricted
   d. evoked

45. After years of experience, Florin became a _____ veterinarian who could treat and operate on many different kinds of animals.
   a. acute
   b. superficial
   c. consummate
   d. ample

46. Anthony, a meticulous young man, _____ watered his neighbor's plants once a week while they were on vacation.
   a. terminally
   b. perpendicularly
   c. diligently
   d. haphazardly

47. _____ elephants from the wild not only endangers the species but upsets the balance of nature.
   a. Irritating
   b. Poaching
   c. Provoking
   d. Smuggling

48. The two cats could be _____ only by the number of rings on their tails; otherwise, they were exactly alike.
   a. separated
   b. divided
   c. disconnected
   d. differentiated

49. On each slick curve in the road, I was afraid we would _____ and have an accident.
   a. operate
   b. hydroplane
   c. submerge
   d. reconnoiter

50. My cousin claimed to be _____; evidently she was right, because she always seemed to know what would happen in the future.
   a. dreamlike
   b. comical
   c. criminal
   d. clairvoyant

ANSWERS

1. **d.** *Incumbent* means the holder of any post or position.
2. **b.** *Demographic* data is the branch of research that deals with human populations.
3. **c.** *Revenue* is the income of a government.
4. **d.** *Blasé* means to be bored or unimpressed by things after having seen or experienced them too often.
5. **b.** The *summit* means the highest point, where the hikers would have a good view.
6. **c.** A *musty* odor is one that is stale or moldy.
7. **a.** *Solitude*, unlike loneliness, can be a desirable thing, and it would be something a person who worked in a busy office would crave.
8. **a.** *Accessible* means capable of being reached or being within easy reach.
9. **d.** *Outmoded* means no longer in style or no longer usable.
10. **b.** A *quest* is a search or pursuit of something, in this case for the perfect cup of coffee.
11. **d.** *Ingenious* means marked by originality, resourcefulness, and cleverness in conception.
12. **a.** An *expressive* person would be one who is open or emphatic when revealing opinions or feelings.
13. **d.** *Favorably* means gracious, kindly, or obliging.
14. **d.** *Docile* means easily led or managed.
15. **c.** *Explicit* means clearly defined.
16. **d.** *Potable* means fit for drinking.
17. **a.** *Encompassed* in this context means included.
18. **b.** *Devised* means to form—in the mind—new combinations or applications of ideas or principles; to plan to obtain or bring about.
19. **c.** *Quandary* means a state of perplexity or doubt.
20. **a.** *Priority* means the right to receive attention before others.
21. **c.** *Conspicuously* means obvious to the eye or mind; attracting attention.
22. **a.** *Monotonous* means having a tedious sameness.
23. **d.** *Resolved* means having reached a firm decision about something.
24. **a.** *Portrayal* means a representation or portrait.
25. **c.** *Careen* means to rush headlong or carelessly; to lurch or swerve while in motion.
26. **d.** *Audibly* means heard or the manner of being heard.
27. **b.** *Voraciously* means having a huge appetite; ravenously.
28. **a.** A *mishap* is an unfortunate accident.
29. **a.** A *rendezvous* is a meeting or assembly that is by appointment or arrangement.
30. **a.** *Warily* is a manner marked by keen caution, cunning, and watchful prudence.
31. **d.** *Legitimate* means in a manner conforming to recognized principles or accepted rules or standards.
32. **b.** *Pummeled* means to pound or beat.
33. **d.** *Facilitate* means to make easier or help to bring about.
34. **c.** *Exemplify* means to be an instance of or serve as an example.

35. b. *Confluence* means a coming or flowing together, a meeting, or a gathering at one point.

36. b. *Replete* means to be filled or abundantly supplied.

37. c. *Convoluted* means presented in a complex and complicated form.

38. d. *Requisite* means essential or necessary.

39. a. *Delude* means to mislead the mind; to deceive.

40. c. *Comprehensive* means covering completely or broadly.

41. b. *Reticent* means inclined to be silent or uncommunicative, reserved.

42. b. *Precursor* means something that comes before.

43. b. *Reputedly* means according to general belief.

44. a. *Abated* means to decrease in force or intensity.

45. c. *Consummate* means extremely skilled and experienced.

46. c. *Diligently* means to do something with careful attention and great effort.

47. b. To *poach* is to trespass on another's property in order to steal fish or game.

48. d. To *differentiate* between two things is to establish the distinction between them.

49. b. When a car goes out of control and skims along the surface of a wet road, it is called *hydroplaning*.

50. d. A *clairvoyant* is someone who can perceive matters beyond the range of ordinary perception.

4

Synonyms and Antonyms

On a Civil Service test, your grasp of the English language will be measured with many different types of vocabulary questions. Frequently, synonym and antonym questions are used to assess your vocabulary aptitude. This chapter covers both of these types of questions. In addition, it provides useful tips and practice exercises that will help you increase your chance of success on this part of the exam.

Acommon measure of verbal skills on standardized tests like a Civil Service exam is the ability to recognize synonyms and antonyms. Synonyms are words that share the same meaning or nearly the same meaning as other words. Antonyms are words with opposite meanings. Test questions often ask you to find the synonym or antonym of a word. If you are lucky, the word will be surrounded by a sentence that helps you guess what the word means (this is vocabulary in context—see Chapter 3), but the test question could list just a synonym or antonym and four answer choices. In this case, you have to figure out what the word means without any help from context clues.

Questions that ask for synonyms and antonyms can be difficult because they require you to have a relatively large vocabulary. Not only do you need to know the word in question, but you may be faced with four choices that are unfamiliar to you, too. Usually the best strategy is to look at the structure of the word. See if a part of the word—the root—looks familiar. Often you will be able to determine the meaning of a word within the root. (See Chapter 2 for a list of word roots.) For instance, the root of credible is *cred*, which means to trust or believe. Knowing this, you will be able to understand the meanings of *incredible*, *sacred*, and *credit*. Looking for related words that have the same root as the word in question can help you choose the correct answer—even if it is by process of elimination.

Another way to dissect meaning is to look for prefixes and suffixes. Prefixes come before the word root, and suffixes are found at the end of a word. Either of these elements can carry meaning or change the use of a word in a sentence. For instance, the prefix can change the meaning of a root word to its opposite: necessary, unnecessary.

A suffix like *less* can change the meaning of a word: *pain* to *painless*. To identify most word parts—word root, prefix, or suffix—the best strategy is to think of words you already know that carry the same root, suffix, or prefix. Let what you know about those words help you find the meaning of words that are less familiar.

Practice

Choose the word or phrase below that best describes the section of the word in bold type.

1. ⓐ ⓑ ⓒ ⓓ
2. ⓐ ⓑ ⓒ ⓓ
3. ⓐ ⓑ ⓒ ⓓ
4. ⓐ ⓑ ⓒ ⓓ
5. ⓐ ⓑ ⓒ ⓓ

1. **pro**active
   a. after
   b. forward
   c. toward
   d. behind

2. in**scribe**
   a. confine
   b. see
   c. perform
   d. write

3. **con**gregation
   a. with
   b. over
   c. apart
   d. time

4. etym**ology**
   a. state of
   b. prior to
   c. study of
   d. quality of

5. wis**dom**

    a. a state of being

    b. a relationship

    c. a property

    d. an action

Answers

    1. b. The prefix *pro-* means *for.* If someone is *proactive,* they are forward thinking and take action or initiative to make things happen.

    2. d. The word root *scribe* means to *write;* to engrave on a surface.

    3. a. The prefix *con-* means to be together with. A *congregation* would gather together with each other.

    4. c. The suffix *-ology* means the study of. *Etymology* is the study of word origins.

    5. a. The suffix *-dom* is a state of being. Someone who has *wisdom* is someone who is wise enough to discern or judge what is right, true, or lasting.

▶ DENOTATION AND CONNOTATION

The *denotation* of a word is simply the dictionary definition. For instance, look at the dictionary definitions for the following words.

    procrastination: to postpone or delay needlessly

    lazy: to be resistant to work or exertion; slow-moving or sluggish

    inactive: not active or tending to be active; not functioning or operating

The *connotation* of a word is its tone. In other words, it is the feeling or emotion you get when you hear a word. Sometimes, the connotation can be favorable or positive. Other times the connotation can be unfavorable or negative. Then again, some words do not arouse any emotion at all and have a neutral connotation.

    Look again at the three words listed above. Their connotations are listed below with an explanation for a favorable, unfavorable, or neutral designation.

    procrastination—favorable. You may have heard people say that they succumbed to procrastination, and that admission is received sympathetically and somewhat approvingly by others because everyone has procrastinated at one time or another. To admit to this trait is considered acceptable.

    lazy—unfavorable. Laziness, which is similar in definition to procrastination, is most assuredly unflattering. The connotation or tone of this word brings up feelings that are definitely unappealing.

inactive—neutral. This word does not elicit any favorable or unfavorable emotions. It is considered a neutral word in this group of three, yet its meaning is similar to the others.

Practice

Read the following sentences three different times using each of the words listed below the sentence. You will note that the sentences take on a new tone and meaning based on each of the words used. Label the words *favorable*, *unfavorable*, or *neutral* based on their connotative meanings.

The keynote speaker for today's meeting plays an _____ role in the political arena.

1. eminent _____
2. infamous _____
3. important _____

The senator _____ the efficiency of the new commerce system in her reelection speech.

4. evaluated _____
5. criticized _____
6. blasted _____

Answers

1. **favorable**. To be *eminent* is considered a good thing. An eminent person is distinguished, well-known, or renowned in a field.
2. **unfavorable**. To be *infamous* is to be famous, but it is fame associated with something dishonorable.
3. **neutral**. To be *important* is to have a high position, yet its connotation does not yield either of the strong feelings of the first two words in this group.
4. **neutral**. To *evaluate* a system suggests a rational and calm exercise. The word does not conjure up negative or positive emotions.
5. **favorable**. To *criticize* a system suggests that the senator is finding fault, yet in the context of this sentence, it is done favorably as part of a bid for reelection.
6. **unfavorable**. To *blast* a system means the senator has unleashed a violent, verbal assault, and this can be viewed unfavorably.

▶ CLARITY

Mark Twain said, "The difference between lightning and the lightning bug is the difference between the right word and the almost right word." Taking this comment into consideration, it is important to know that there are often many synonyms for one word. It is essential to be as clear as possible when choosing synonyms. While some synonyms can be similar, they are rarely identical. For instance, the words *bountiful, ample, plentiful,* and *glut* suggest abundance. However, one of these words suggests an overabundance. While you can have a bountiful, ample, or plentiful supply of food on the table for

Thanksgiving dinner, a glut of food is an excessive amount of food that suggests there will be waste involved. It is important to choose your words carefully. Note the similarities in the questions below to see the importance of using just the right word.

Practice

Choose the clearest synonym for each of the following questions.

1. Their conversation was considered playful _____ between two old friends.
   a. antics
   b. banter
   c. behavior
   d. activities

2. He tried to _____ the morale of his friend in the hospital.
   a. sustain
   b. foster
   c. bolster
   d. nourish

Answers

1. **b.** *Banter* is defined as remarks or talk that are playful and teasing. Choice **a** is incorrect because antics are unpredictable behavior or actions. Choices **c** and **d** are incorrect because their definitions are too broad and do not focus on conversation.

2. **c.** Bolster (choice **c**) and sustain (choice **a**) can both be defined as supporting, but the fine difference between the two is in the fact that bolster means to boost, whereas sustain means to keep something at an existing level. Choices **b** and **d** are incorrect because they do not mean to boost or raise.

Synonym Practice

In the following questions, identify the correct synonym by looking for word roots, prefixes, suffixes, or definitions. Choose the word that means the same or about the same as the italicized word. Look for answers and explanations at the end of the practice.

1. a *partial* report
   a. identifiable
   b. incomplete
   c. visible
   d. enhanced

2. a *substantial* report
   a. inconclusive
   b. weighty
   c. proven
   d. alleged

3. *corroborate* the statement
   a. confirm
   b. negate
   c. deny
   d. challenge

4. *manufactured* goods
   a. reverted
   b. transgressed
   c. regressed
   d. processed

5. an *incoherent* answer
   a. not understandable
   b. not likely
   c. undeniable
   d. challenging

6. covered with *debris*
   a. good excuses
   b. transparent material
   c. scattered rubble
   d. protective material

7. *inadvertently* left
   a. mistakenly
   b. purposely
   c. cautiously
   d. carefully

8. *compatible* workers
   a. gifted
   b. competitive
   c. harmonious
   d. experienced

Answers

1. **b.** *Partial* means *incomplete*. The root of the word here is *part*. A partial report is only part of the whole.

2. **b.** A *substantial* report is extensive. The key part of the word substantial is *substance*. Substance means something that has significance.

3. **a.** To *corroborate* is to *confirm*. Notice the prefix *co-*, which means with or together. Some related words are *cooperate*, *coworker*, and *collide*. *Corroboration* means that one statement fits with another.

4. **d.** *Manufactured* goods are those that are made or processed from raw material into a finished product. *Facer*—the word root—means to make or do.

5. **a.** *Incoherent* means *not understandable*. To *cohere* means to *connect*. A coherent answer connects or makes sense. The prefix *in* means not.

6. **c.** *Debris* is scattered fragments or trash.

7. **a.** *Inadvertently* means *by mistake*. The key element in this word is the prefix *in*, which means not.

8. **c.** *Compatible* means capable of existing or performing in *harmony*.

Antonym Practice

Antonym questions can be problematic because you can easily forget that you are looking for *opposites* and mistakenly choose the synonym. Very often, synonyms will be included as answer choices for antonym questions. The trick is to keep your mind on the fact that you are looking for the opposite of the word given in the question. If you are allowed to mark in your test booklet or on the test paper, circle the word *antonym* or *opposite* in the directions to help you remember.

Otherwise, the same tactics that work for synonym questions work for antonyms as well. Try to determine the meaning of part of the word, or try to remember a context where you have seen the word before.

Choose the word that means the opposite of the italicized word in the questions below. Look for answers and explanations at the end of the practice.

9. *prompt* payment
    a. punctual
    b. slack
    c. tardy
    d. regular

10. *delay* the decision
    a. slow
    b. hasten
    c. pause
    d. desist

11. *moderate* work flow
   a. original
   b. average
   c. final
   d. excessive

12. *initial* impression
   a. first
   b. crisis
   c. final
   d. right

13. *capable* employee
   a. unskilled
   b. absurd
   c. apt
   d. able

14. *zealous* pursuit
   a. envious
   b. eager
   c. idle
   d. comical

15. *exorbitant* prices
   a. expensive
   b. unexpected
   c. reasonable
   d. outrageous

16. *belligerent* attitude
   a. hostile
   b. appeasing
   c. instinctive
   d. ungracious

Answers

9. **c.** The key here is to remember not to choose the synonym. Context clues are important as well. You may have seen this sentence on one of your bills: *Prompt* payment is appreciated. *Prompt* means punctual; *tardy* means late.

10. **b.** To *delay* is to postpone. If a decision is delayed, it will happen more slowly. To *delay* is to slow; to *hasten* is to hurry.

11. d. Something that is moderate is not subject to extremes. *Moderate* means average; *excessive* means extreme.

12. c. An initial impression is one that comes first. *Initial* means first; *final* means last.

13. a. The suffix *-able* tells you that a capable employee is one who has ability. *Capable* means able; *unskilled* means unable.

14. c. *Zealous* means *eager*, so *idle* is most nearly the opposite. You may have heard the word *zeal* before, which might give you a clue about the meaning of the word. One other precaution is to be careful and not be misled by the similar sounds of *zealous* and *jealous*. The other trick is not to choose the synonym, eager, choice **b.**

15. c. The best clue in this word is the prefix *ex*, which means *out of* or *away from*. *Exorbitant* literally means *exceeding the bounds of what is fair or normal; very high*. The opposite of an *exorbitant* or *outrageous* price would be a *reasonable* one.

16. b. The key element in this word is the root *belli-*, which means *warlike*. The synonym choices—*hostile* and *ungracious*—are incorrect. The antonym would be *appeasing*.

PRACTICE QUESTIONS

The 50 questions in this exercise are a mix of synonyms and antonyms. Select the synonym or antonym for the word in italics according to the directions in each question. Use this answer grid to fill in your answers to the questions.

1.	ⓐ	ⓑ	ⓒ	ⓓ	26.	ⓐ	ⓑ	ⓒ	ⓓ
2.	ⓐ	ⓑ	ⓒ	ⓓ	27.	ⓐ	ⓑ	ⓒ	ⓓ
3.	ⓐ	ⓑ	ⓒ	ⓓ	28.	ⓐ	ⓑ	ⓒ	ⓓ
4.	ⓐ	ⓑ	ⓒ	ⓓ	29.	ⓐ	ⓑ	ⓒ	ⓓ
5.	ⓐ	ⓑ	ⓒ	ⓓ	30.	ⓐ	ⓑ	ⓒ	ⓓ
6.	ⓐ	ⓑ	ⓒ	ⓓ	31.	ⓐ	ⓑ	ⓒ	ⓓ
7.	ⓐ	ⓑ	ⓒ	ⓓ	32.	ⓐ	ⓑ	ⓒ	ⓓ
8.	ⓐ	ⓑ	ⓒ	ⓓ	33.	ⓐ	ⓑ	ⓒ	ⓓ
9.	ⓐ	ⓑ	ⓒ	ⓓ	34.	ⓐ	ⓑ	ⓒ	ⓓ
10.	ⓐ	ⓑ	ⓒ	ⓓ	35.	ⓐ	ⓑ	ⓒ	ⓓ
11.	ⓐ	ⓑ	ⓒ	ⓓ	36.	ⓐ	ⓑ	ⓒ	ⓓ
12.	ⓐ	ⓑ	ⓒ	ⓓ	37.	ⓐ	ⓑ	ⓒ	ⓓ
13.	ⓐ	ⓑ	ⓒ	ⓓ	38.	ⓐ	ⓑ	ⓒ	ⓓ
14.	ⓐ	ⓑ	ⓒ	ⓓ	39.	ⓐ	ⓑ	ⓒ	ⓓ
15.	ⓐ	ⓑ	ⓒ	ⓓ	40.	ⓐ	ⓑ	ⓒ	ⓓ
16.	ⓐ	ⓑ	ⓒ	ⓓ	41.	ⓐ	ⓑ	ⓒ	ⓓ
17.	ⓐ	ⓑ	ⓒ	ⓓ	42.	ⓐ	ⓑ	ⓒ	ⓓ
18.	ⓐ	ⓑ	ⓒ	ⓓ	43.	ⓐ	ⓑ	ⓒ	ⓓ
19.	ⓐ	ⓑ	ⓒ	ⓓ	44.	ⓐ	ⓑ	ⓒ	ⓓ
20.	ⓐ	ⓑ	ⓒ	ⓓ	45.	ⓐ	ⓑ	ⓒ	ⓓ
21.	ⓐ	ⓑ	ⓒ	ⓓ	46.	ⓐ	ⓑ	ⓒ	ⓓ
22.	ⓐ	ⓑ	ⓒ	ⓓ	47.	ⓐ	ⓑ	ⓒ	ⓓ
23.	ⓐ	ⓑ	ⓒ	ⓓ	48.	ⓐ	ⓑ	ⓒ	ⓓ
24.	ⓐ	ⓑ	ⓒ	ⓓ	49.	ⓐ	ⓑ	ⓒ	ⓓ
25.	ⓐ	ⓑ	ⓒ	ⓓ	50.	ⓐ	ⓑ	ⓒ	ⓓ

1. A synonym for *vast* is
   a. attentive.
   b. immense.
   c. steady.
   d. slight.

2. A synonym for *enthusiastic* is
   a. adamant.
   c. available.
   d. cheerful.
   b. eager.

3. A synonym for *adequate* is
   a. sufficient.
   b. mediocre.
   c. proficient.
   d. average.

4. A synonym for *comply* is
   a. subdue.
   b. entertain.
   c. flatter.
   d. obey.

5. An antonym for *uniform* is
   a. dissembling.
   b. diverse.
   c. bizarre.
   d. slovenly.

6. A synonym for *ecstatic* is
   a. inconsistent.
   b. positive.
   c. wild.
   d. thrilled.

7. A synonym for *affect* is
   a. accomplish.
   b. cause.
   c. sicken.
   d. influence.

8. An antonym for *wary* is
   a. alert.
   b. leery.
   c. worried.
   d. careless.

9. An antonym for *novel* is
   a. dangerous.
   b. unsettled.
   c. suitable.
   d. old.

10. A synonym for *continuous* is
   a. intermittent.
   b. adjacent.
   c. uninterrupted.
   d. contiguous.

11. A synonym for *courtesy* is
   a. civility.
   b. congruity.
   c. conviviality.
   d. rudeness.

12. An antonym for *fallacy* is
   a. truth.
   b. blessing.
   c. weakness.
   d. fable.

13. An antonym for *optimum* is
   a. mediocre.
   b. victorious.
   c. worst.
   d. rational.

14. A synonym for *frail* is
   a. vivid.
   b. delicate.
   c. robust.
   d. adaptable.

15. A synonym for *recuperate* is
   a. mend.
   b. endorse.
   c. persist.
   d. worsen.

16. An antonym for *subsequent* is
   a. necessary.
   b. insignificant.
   c. primary.
   d. previous.

17. A synonym for *enlighten* is
   a. relocate.
   b. confuse.
   c. comply.
   d. teach.

18. A synonym for *garnish* is
   a. depart.
   b. please.
   c. tarnish.
   d. embellish.

19. A synonym for *composure* is
   a. agitation.
   b. poise.
   c. liveliness.
   d. stimulation.

20. A synonym for *verify* is
   a. disclose.
   b. confirm.
   c. refute.
   d. unite.

21. An antonym for *disperse* is
   a. gather.
   b. agree.
   c. praise.
   d. satisfy.

22. A synonym for *eccentric* is
   a. normal.
   b. frugal.
   c. peculiar.
   d. selective.

23. A synonym for *commendable* is
   a. admirable.
   b. accountable.
   c. irresponsible.
   d. noticeable.

24. An antonym for *pacify* is
   a. complicate.
   b. dismiss.
   c. excite.
   d. atomize.

25. An antonym for *mirth* is
   a. height.
   b. solemnity.
   c. expense.
   d. preparation.

26. A synonym for *domain* is
   a. entrance.
   b. rebellion.
   c. formation.
   d. territory.

27. A synonym for *passive* is
   a. inactive.
   b. emotional.
   c. lively.
   d. woeful.

28. An antonym for *liberate* is
   a. conserve.
   b. restrain.
   c. attack.
   d. ruin.

29. An antonym for *faltering* is
   a. steady.
   b. adoring.
   c. explanatory.
   d. reluctant.

30. An antonym for *succinct* is
   a. laconic.
   b. feeble.
   c. verbose.
   d. attentive.

31. An antonym for *tedious* is
   a. stimulating.
   b. alarming.
   c. intemperate.
   d. tranquil.

32. An antonym for *exonerate* is
   a. minimize.
   b. respect.
   c. irritate.
   d. blame.

33. An antonym for *ephemeral* is
   a. internal.
   b. enduring.
   c. temporary.
   d. hidden.

34. An antonym for *nonchalant* is
   a. intelligent.
   b. popular.
   c. concerned.
   d. reckless.

35. A synonym for *rigorous* is
   a. demanding.
   b. tolerable.
   c. lenient.
   d. disorderly.

36. An antonym for *orient* is
   a. confuse.
   b. arouse.
   c. deter.
   d. simplify.

37. An antonym for *levitate* is
   a. plod.
   b. undulate.
   c. whisper.
   d. sink.

38. A synonym for *oblivious* is
   a. visible.
   b. sinister.
   c. conscious.
   d. unaware.

39. An antonym for *excise* is
   a. sleep.
   b. retain.
   c. organize.
   d. staple.

40. An antonym for *prevarication* is
   a. ignorance.
   b. veracity.
   c. courtesy.
   d. serenity.

41. An antonym for *plausible* is
   a. insufficient.
   b. apologetic.
   c. unbelievable.
   d. credible.

42. A synonym for *rational* is
  a. deliberate.
  b. invalid.
  c. prompt.
  d. sound.

43. A synonym for *idle* is
  a. working.
  b. effective.
  c. immobile.
  d. functional.

44. An antonym for *avid* is
  a. partial.
  b. unenthusiastic.
  c. equal.
  d. unkind.

45. An antonym for *meek* is
  a. mild.
  b. painful.
  c. forceful.
  d. polite.

46. A synonym for *attribute* is
  a. quality.
  b. penalty.
  c. speech.
  d. admission.

47. A synonym for *subdue* is
  a. conquer.
  b. complain.
  c. deny.
  d. respect.

48. An antonym for *complacent* is
   a. concerned.
   b. pleasant.
   c. happy.
   d. convinced.

49. An antonym for *ambiguous* is
   a. apathetic.
   b. certain.
   c. equivocal.
   d. indefinite.

50. A synonym for *confer* is
   a. confide.
   b. consult.
   c. refuse.
   d. promise.

ANSWERS

1. b. *Vast* means very great in size; *immense*.

2. d. *Enthusiastic* means *eager*.

3. a. If something is *adequate*, it is *sufficient*.

4. d. *Comply* is synonymous with *obey*.

5. b. To be *uniform* is be consistent or the same as others; to be *diverse* is to have variety.

6. d. A person who is *ecstatic* is *thrilled*.

7. d. To *affect* means to *influence*.

8. d. To be *wary* is to be on guard or watchful; *careless* is the opposite of watchful.

9. d. To be novel is to be *new*; the opposite is *old*.

10. c. *Continuous* means marked by *uninterrupted* extension in space and time.

11. a. A *courtesy* is a courteous or mannerly act; it is characterized by *civility*.

12. a. A *fallacy* is a false or mistaken idea, trickery; a *truth* is something which conforms to the facts.

13. c. *Optimum* means the most *desirable*; *worst* means the least desirable or good.

14. b. A *frail* person is weak and *delicate*.

15. a. *Recuperate* means to heal or *mend*.

16. d. *Subsequent* means coming after or following; *previous* means coming before.

17. d. If you *enlighten* someone, you instruct, inform, or *teach* to make them free of ignorance, prejudice or superstition.

18. d. To *garnish* means to adorn, decorate or embellish.

19. b. If you have *composure* and are self-assured, calm, or tranquil, you have *poise*.

20. b. To *verify* means to establish the truth or accuracy; to *confirm*.

21. a. *Disperse* means to scatter; to *gather* means to collect in one place.

22. c. An *eccentric* person is considered to be odd or *peculiar*.

23. a. *Commendable* is the same as *admirable*.

24. c. To *pacify* means to calm; to *excite* means to stir up.

25. b. *Mirth* means merriment; *solemnity* means seriousness.

26. d. A *domain* is an area governed by a ruler; a *territory* is an area for which someone is responsible.

27. a. To be *passive* is to accept or submit without rejection or resistance, or to be *inactive*.

28. b. To *liberate* means to release; to *restrain* means to deprive of liberty.

29. a. *Faltering* means stumbling, unsteady; *steady* means unfaltering, fixed or secure.

30. c. To be *succinct* is to be *concise*; to be *verbose* is to be *wordy*.

31. a. To be *tedious* is to be *tiresome*; to be *stimulating* is to be *exciting*.

32. d. To *exonerate* means to clear from accusation or guilt; to *blame* is to accuse or hold responsible.

33. b. *Ephemeral* means short-lived; *enduring* means without end.

34. c. To be *nonchalant* means to have an air of easy indifference; to be *concerned* means to be interested and involved.

35. **a.** *Rigorous* is synonymous with *demanding*.

36. **a.** To *orient* means to adjust, become familiar; to *confuse* means to bewilder.

37. **d.** To *levitate* means to rise and float; to *sink* means to submerge or descend to the bottom.

38. **d.** If you are *oblivious* to your surroundings, you are *unaware* of them.

39. **b.** To *excise* means to remove; to *retain* means to keep.

40. **b.** A *prevarication* is an evasion of the truth; *veracity* is truthfulness.

41. **c.** *Plausible* means likely; *unbelievable* is unlikely.

42. **d.** A *rational* decision is a *sound* or reasonable decision.

43. **c.** *Idle* is synonymous with *immobile*, meaning not moving, still.

44. **b.** *Avid* means characterized by enthusiasm and vigorous pursuit; the opposite would be *unenthusiastic*.

45. **c.** *Meek* means not violent or not strong; *forceful* means powerful.

46. **a.** An *attribute* is a characteristic or *quality* belonging to a person or thing.

47. **a.** To *subdue* means to bring under control; *conquer*.

48. **a.** *Complacent* means self-satisfied, smug, or unworried; the opposite is *concerned*.

49. **b.** To be *ambiguous* is to be equivocal or obscure; to be *certain* is to be definite or fixed.

50. **b.** *Confer* means to compare views or to take counsel; *consult*.

CHAPTER

5

Reading Comprehension

Because understanding what you read is such a vital skill, most Civil Service exams include a reading comprehension section that tests your ability to understand what you read. To read effectively, you should be able to find the main idea of a passage, select the topic sentence, locate basic support material or details, discern fact from opinion, and make inferences. This chapter reviews each of these skills.

The reading comprehension portion of the written test is usually presented as a multiple-choice test and will ask questions based on brief passages, much like the standardized tests you probably took in school. Reading comprehension questions offer you two advantages as a test taker. First, you do not need any prior knowledge about the topic of the passage. Second, you will be tested only on the information presented in the passage. The disadvantage is that you have to know where and how to find the information you need under certain time constraints and in an unfamiliar text. This somewhat stressful combination makes it easy to choose one of the wrong answer choices, especially since the choices are deliberately designed to mislead you. If you are in a hurry, it is easy to make a mistake.

As you study this reading comprehension section, understand that your vocabulary skills play a vital role when you have to decipher any written text. Sometimes, just one difficult word can skew your understanding of a sentence. Two or three unknown words can make a passage difficult, or even impossible, to interpret. It is important to understand that the study of vocabulary in combination with reading comprehension go hand in hand as you continue your test preparation.

The best way to do well on a reading comprehension test is to be very familiar with the kinds of questions that are typically asked, and then to know how to respond to these questions. Questions most frequently ask you to:

▶ determine the main idea of the passage.

▶ identify a specific fact or detail in the passage.

▶ identify the topic sentence.

▶ discern fact from opinion.

▶ make an inference based on the passage.

▶ define a vocabulary word from the passage. (Refer to Chapter 3 to practice this skill.)

Once you know the kinds of questions that will be asked, you can develop some strategies to help you choose correct answers. To do this, you must be a discriminating reader and know where to look for the information, facts, and details you need to help you choose correctly.

One strategy used by many readers is highlighting and underlining. By highlighting or underlining key words and phrases, you can make important details stand out. This helps you quickly find the information later when you need to answer a question or write a summary. To highlight key words and ideas, you must be able to determine which facts and ideas are most important.

Here are three guidelines for highlighting or underlining your text.

1. **Be selective.** If you highlight four sentences in a five-sentence paragraph, this will not help you. The key is to identify what is most important in the paragraph. Ask yourself two questions:
   ▶What is the main point the author is trying to make—what is the main idea of the paragraph?
   ▶What information is emphasized or seems to stand out as especially important?
2. **Watch for word clues.** Certain words and phrases indicate that key information will follow. Words and phrases such as *most important, the key is,* and *significantly* are clues to watch out for.
3. **Watch for visual clues.** Key words and ideas are often boldfaced, underlined, or italicized. They may be boxed or repeated in a sidebar as well.

For practice, read the following paragraph and answer the questions that follow. The answer explanation following each type of question—main idea, detail/support material, topic sentence, fact/opinion, and inference—will point out reading comprehension strategies that help you choose the correct answer.

Today's postal service is more efficient and reliable than ever before. Mail that used to take months to move by horse and by foot now moves around the country in days or hours by truck, train, and plane. First class mail usually moves from New York City to Los Angeles in three days or less. If your letter or package is urgent, the U.S. Postal Service offers Priority Mail and Express Mail services. Priority Mail is guaranteed to go anywhere in the United States in two days or less. Express Mail will get your package there overnight, or your money will be refunded. Additionally, the U.S. Postal Service offers lower rates for the same services offered by many competitors.

Main Idea Question

1. What is the main idea of this paragraph?
    a. The post office offers many services.
    b. Express Mail is a good way to send urgent mail.
    c. First class mail usually takes three days or less.
    d. Mail service today is more effective and dependable.

If you selected choice **a**, you would be choosing the subject of the paragraph, not the main idea. The main idea must say something about the subject. To accurately find the main idea of a text, remember that it is usually an *assertion* about the subject. An assertion is a statement that requires evidence or proof to be accepted as true. While the main idea of a passage is an assertion about its subject, it is something more. It is the idea that holds together or controls the passage. The other sentences and ideas in the passage will all relate to that main idea and serve as evidence that the assertion is true.

You might think of the main idea as an umbrella that is held over the other sentences. It must be *general* enough or big enough to cover all of these ideas underneath it (in the paragraph or passage). Choice **b** is too specific to be the main idea; it tells you only about Express Mail. It does not include any information about Priority Mail or first class mail, so it cannot be the main idea of the paragraph. Choice **c** is also too specific. It tells you about first class mail only, so this choice can be excluded. Choice **d** is general enough to encompass the entire passage. The rest of the sentences in the paragraph support the idea that this sentence asserts. Each sentence offers proof that the postal expresses the writer's purpose—to show the efficiency and reliability of today's postal service.

Fact/Detail Question

2. Today's mail is transported by
    a. foot.
    b. horse.
    c. trucks, trains, and planes.
    d. overnight services.

Choices **a** and **b** are mentioned in the paragraph, and you may mistakenly choose one of these if you only scan the paragraph quickly. However, if you read more closely, you will see that in the past, "Mail used to take months to move by horse and by foot," but it "now moves around the country in days or hours by truck, train, and plane," choice **c**. Choice **d** is a misleading answer. Overnight mail services are transported by truck, train, and plane as well.

Topic Sentence Question

3. Of the following sentences, which one is the topic sentence?
   a. Mail that used to take months to move by horse and by foot now moves around the country in days or hours by truck, train, and plane.
   b. Today's postal service is more efficient and reliable than ever before.
   c. If your letter or package is urgent, the U.S. Postal Service offers Priority Mail and Express Mail services.
   d. Express Mail will get your package there overnight.

You will notice that in the paragraph, the main idea is expressed clearly in the first sentence, choice **b**. A sentence such as this one that clearly expresses the main idea of a paragraph or passage is called the *topic sentence*. In many cases, you will find the topic sentence at the beginning of the paragraph, but this is not a hard and fast rule. The topic sentence can be found in the middle or at the end of a paragraph. However, for the sentence to be labeled a topic sentence, it must be an assertion, and it needs proof. The proof is found in the facts and ideas that make up the rest of the paragraph. Choices **a**, **c**, and **d** are sentences that offer specific facts and ideas that support choice **b**.

Fact/Opinion Question

4. "Express Mail will get your package there overnight, or your money will be refunded." This statement is a/an
   a. fact.
   b. opinion.

Facts are things known for certain to have happened, to be true, or to exist. Opinions are things believed to have happened, believed to be true, or believed to exist. As you can see, the key difference between fact and opinion lies in the distinction between believing and knowing. Opinions may be based on facts, but they are still what we think, not what we know. Opinions are debatable; facts are not. The statement in the question, "Express Mail will get your package there overnight or your money will be refunded," is a fact, choice **a**.

Inference Question

5. Based on the information in the paragraph, it is safe to say that
   a. it is economical for businesses to take advantage of Express Mail services.
   b. the old fashioned pony express system of mail delivery did not work.
   c. first class mail service is unreliable.
   d. there is no way to deliver urgent mail.

An inference is a conclusion that can be drawn based on fact or evidence. You can infer that businesses could take advantage of Express Mail service to speed up deliveries, choice **a**, based on the evidence in the paragraph. "Express Mail will get your package there overnight," justifiably supports this inference. Choices **b**, **c**, and **d** cannot be inferred based on any concrete evidence from the paragraph.

Knowing that reading comprehension questions can include main idea, topic sentence, detail, fact/opinion, or inference questions is a practical beginning for reading comprehension skills. Add a few test strategies—knowing where and how to look for the information, facts, and details—and you will feel comfortable and confident when it comes time to take the test.

PRACTICE QUESTIONS

Read the following paragraphs and answer the reading comprehension questions based on your knowledge of the main idea of each paragraph Use this answer grid to fill in your answers to the questions.

1.	ⓐ	ⓑ	ⓒ	ⓓ		26.	ⓐ	ⓑ	ⓒ	ⓓ
2.	ⓐ	ⓑ	ⓒ	ⓓ		27.	ⓐ	ⓑ	ⓒ	ⓓ
3.	ⓐ	ⓑ	ⓒ	ⓓ		28.	ⓐ	ⓑ	ⓒ	ⓓ
4.	ⓐ	ⓑ	ⓒ	ⓓ		29.	Ⓕ	Ⓞ		
5.	ⓐ	ⓑ	ⓒ	ⓓ		30.	Ⓕ	Ⓞ		
6.	ⓐ	ⓑ	ⓒ	ⓓ		31.	Ⓕ	Ⓞ		
7.	ⓐ	ⓑ	ⓒ	ⓓ		32.	Ⓕ	Ⓞ		
8.	ⓐ	ⓑ	ⓒ	ⓓ		33.	Ⓕ	Ⓞ		
9.	ⓐ	ⓑ	ⓒ	ⓓ		34.	Ⓕ	Ⓞ		
10.	ⓐ	ⓑ	ⓒ	ⓓ		35.	Ⓕ	Ⓞ		
11.	ⓐ	ⓑ	ⓒ	ⓓ		36.	Ⓕ	Ⓞ		
12.	ⓐ	ⓑ	ⓒ	ⓓ		37.	Ⓕ	Ⓞ		
13.	ⓐ	ⓑ	ⓒ	ⓓ		38.	Ⓕ	Ⓞ		
14.	ⓐ	ⓑ	ⓒ	ⓓ		39.	ⓐ	ⓑ	ⓒ	ⓓ
15.	ⓐ	ⓑ	ⓒ	ⓓ		40.	ⓐ	ⓑ	ⓒ	ⓓ
16.	ⓐ	ⓑ	ⓒ	ⓓ		41.	ⓐ	ⓑ	ⓒ	ⓓ
17.	ⓐ	ⓑ	ⓒ	ⓓ		42.	ⓐ	ⓑ	ⓒ	ⓓ
18.	ⓐ	ⓑ	ⓒ	ⓓ		43.	ⓐ	ⓑ	ⓒ	ⓓ
19.	ⓐ	ⓑ	ⓒ	ⓓ		44.	ⓐ	ⓑ	ⓒ	ⓓ
20.	ⓐ	ⓑ	ⓒ	ⓓ		45.	ⓐ	ⓑ	ⓒ	ⓓ
21.	ⓐ	ⓑ	ⓒ	ⓓ		46.	ⓐ	ⓑ	ⓒ	ⓓ
22.	ⓐ	ⓑ	ⓒ	ⓓ		47.	ⓐ	ⓑ	ⓒ	ⓓ
23.	ⓐ	ⓑ	ⓒ	ⓓ		48.	ⓐ	ⓑ	ⓒ	ⓓ
24.	ⓐ	ⓑ	ⓒ	ⓓ		49.	ⓐ	ⓑ	ⓒ	ⓓ
25.	ⓐ	ⓑ	ⓒ	ⓓ		50.	ⓐ	ⓑ	ⓒ	ⓓ

If you are a fitness walker, there is no need for a commute to a health club. Your neighborhood can be your health club. You do not need a lot of fancy equipment to get a good workout, either. All you need is a well-designed pair of athletic shoes.

   1. This paragraph best supports the statement that
      a. fitness walking is a better form of exercise than weight lifting.
      b. a membership in a health club is a poor investment.
      c. walking outdoors provides a better workout than walking indoors.
      d. fitness walking is a convenient and valuable form of exercise.

Critical reading is a demanding process. To read critically, you must slow down your reading and, with pencil in hand, perform specific operations on the text. Mark up the text with your reactions, conclusions, and questions. In other words, when you read, become an active participant.

   2. This paragraph best supports the statement that
      a. critical reading is a slow, dull, but essential process.
      b. the best critical reading happens at critical times in a person's life.
      c. readers should get in the habit of questioning the truth of what they read.
      d. critical reading requires thoughtful and careful attention.

One New York publisher has estimated that 50,000 to 60,000 people in the United States want an anthology that includes the complete works of William Shakespeare. What accounts for this renewed interest in Shakespeare? As scholars point out, his psychological insights into both male and female characters are amazing, even today.

   3. This paragraph best supports the statement that
      a. Shakespeare's characters are more interesting than fictional characters today.
      b. people today are interested in Shakespeare's work because of the characters.
      c. academic scholars are putting together an anthology of Shakespeare's work.
      d. New Yorkers have a renewed interest in the work of Shakespeare.

There are no effective boundaries when it comes to pollutants. Studies have shown that toxic insecticides—already banned in many countries—are riding the wind from countries where they remain legal. Compounds such as DDT and toxaphene have been found in remote places like the Yukon and other Arctic regions.

   4. This paragraph best supports the statement that
      a. bans on toxins have done little to stop the spread of pollutants.
      b. more pollutants find their way into polar climates than they do into warmer areas.
      c. studies show that many countries have ignored their own anti-pollution laws.
      d. DDT and toxaphene are the two most toxic insecticides in the world.

The Fourth Amendment to the Constitution protects citizens against unreasonable searches and seizures. No search of a person's home or personal effects may be conducted without a written search warrant issued on probable cause. This means that a neutral judge must approve the factual basis justifying a search before it can be conducted.

5. This paragraph best supports the statement that police officers cannot search a person's home or private papers unless they have

   a. legal authorization.

   b. direct evidence of a crime.

   c. read the person his or her constitutional rights.

   d. a reasonable belief that a crime has occurred.

Mathematics allows us to expand our consciousness. Mathematics tells us about economic trends, patterns of disease, and the growth of populations. Math is good at exposing the truth, but it can also perpetuate misunderstandings and untruths. Figures have the power to mislead people.

6. This paragraph best supports the statement that

   a. the study of mathematics is dangerous.

   b. the study of mathematics can be both beneficial and confusing.

   c. the study of mathematics is more important than other disciplines.

   d. the power of numbers is that they cannot lie.

Human technology began with the development of the first stone tools about two and a half million years ago. In the beginning, the rate of development was slow, and hundreds of thousands of years passed without many technological changes. Today, new technologies are reported daily on television and in newspapers.

7. This paragraph best supports the statement that

   a. stone tools were not really technology.

   b. stone tools were in use for two and a half million years.

   c. there is no way to know when stone tools first came into use.

   d. in today's world, new technologies are constantly being developed.

Read the following paragraphs and choose the correct fact or detail to answer the questions.

Ratatouille is a dish that has grown in popularity over the last few years. It features eggplant, zucchini, tomato, peppers, and garlic chopped, mixed, sautéed, and finally, cooked slowly over low heat. As the vegetables cook slowly, they make their own broth, and this can be extended with a little tomato paste. The name *ratatouille* comes from the French word *touiller*, meaning to mix or stir together.

8. Which of the following is the correct order of steps for making ratatouille?

   a. Chop vegetables, add tomato paste, and stir or mix together.

   b. Mix the vegetables together, sauté them, and add tomato paste.

   c. Cook the vegetables slowly, mix them together, and add tomato paste.

   d. Add tomato paste to extend the broth and cook slowly over low heat.

9. Ratatouille can best be described as a
   a. French pastry.
   b. sauce to put over vegetables.
   c. pasta dish extended with tomato paste.
   d. vegetable stew.

After a snow or ice fall, the city streets are treated with ordinary rock salt. In some areas, the salt is combined with calcium chloride, which is more effective in below-zero temperatures and which melts ice better. This combination of salt and calcium chloride is also less damaging to foliage along the roadways.

10. In deciding whether to use ordinary rock salt or the salt and calcium chloride mixture on a particular street, which of the following is *not* a consideration?
    a. the temperature at the time of treatment
    b. the plants and trees along the street
    c. whether there is ice on the street
    d. whether the street is a main or secondary road

11. According to the snow treatment information in the paragraph above, which of the following is true?
    a. If the temperature is below zero, a salt and calcium chloride mixture is effective in treating snow and ice-covered streets.
    b. Crews must wait until the snow or ice stops falling before salting streets.
    c. Major roads are always salted first.
    d. If the snowfall is light, the city road crews will not salt the streets because this would be a waste of the salt supply.

Many cities have distributed standardized recycling containers to all households. One city attached the following directions: We prefer that you use this new container as your primary recycling container, as this will expedite pickup of recyclables. Additional recycling containers may be purchased as needed from the Sanitation Department.

12. According to the directions, each household
    a. may use only one recycling container.
    b. must use the new recycling container.
    c. should use the new recycling container.
    d. must buy a new recycling container.

13. According to the directions in the paragraph above, which of the following is true about the new containers?
    a. The new containers are far better than other containers in every way.
    b. The new containers will help increase the efficiency of the recycling program.
    c. The new containers hold more than the old containers did.
    d. The new containers are less expensive than the old.

Read the following paragraphs and choose the topic sentence that best fits the paragraph.

Spices is a pleasant word, whether it connotes fine French cuisine or down-home cinnamon-flavored apple pie. _____. In the past, individuals traveled the world seeking exotic spices for profit and, in searching, have changed the course of history. Indeed, to gain control of lands harboring new spices, nations have actually gone to war.

14. **a.** The taste and aroma of spices are the main elements that make food such a source or fascination and pleasure.

  b. The term might equally bring to mind Indian curry made thousands of miles away or those delicious barbecued ribs sold down at Harry's.

  c. It is exciting to find a good cookbook and experiment with spices from other lands—indeed, it is one way to travel around the globe.

  d. The history of spices, however, is another matter altogether, and it can be filled with danger and intrigue.

It weighs less than three pounds and is hardly more interesting to look at than an overly ripe cauliflower. _____. It has created poetry and music, planned and executed wars, devised intricate scientific theories. It thinks and dreams, plots and schemes, and easily holds more information than all the libraries on earth.

15. **a.** The human brain is made of gelatinous matter and contains no nerve endings.

  b. The science of neurology has found a way to map the most important areas of the human brain.

  c. Nevertheless, the human brain is the most mysterious and complex object on earth.

  d. However, scientists say that each person uses only 10% of brainpower over the course of a lifetime.

Gary is a very distinguished looking man with a touch of gray at the temples. Even in his early fifties, he is still the one to turn heads. He enjoys spending most of his time admiring his profile in the mirror. In fact, he considers his good looks to be his second-most important asset in the world. The first, however, is money. He was fortunate enough to be born into a wealthy family, and he loves the power his wealth has given him. _____. He can buy whatever he desires. Gary checks the mirror often and feels great delight with what he sees.

16. **a.** Gary's gray hair is his worst characteristic.

  b. Conceit is the beginning and the end of Gary's character; conceit of person and situation.

  c. Gary feels blessed to be wealthy and the joy consumes his every thought.

  d. The only objects of Gary's respect are others who hold positions in society above him.

Read the following topic sentences and choose the sentence that best develops or supports the topic sentence.

17. Life on earth is ancient, and at its first appearance, unimaginably complex.

   a. Scientists place its beginnings at some three billion years ago, when the first molecule floated up out of the ooze with the unique ability to replicate itself.

   b. The most complex life form is, of course, the mammal—and the most complex mammal is humankind.

   c. It is unknown exactly where life started—where the first molecule was "born" that had the ability to replicate itself.

   d. Darwin's theory of evolution was one attempt to explain what essentially remains a great mystery.

18. The continuing fascination of the public with movie star Marilyn Monroe is puzzling, yet it is still strong, even after many decades.

   a. She became a star in the 1950s and died in 1962.

   b. The film that most clearly demonstrates her talent is *The Misfits*.

   c. Her name was originally Norma Jean, but she changed it to Marilyn.

   d. One reason might simply be her life's sad and premature end.

19. One scientific theory of the origin of the universe is the much misunderstood big-bang theory.

   a. Physicists now believe they can construct what happened in the universe during the first three minutes of its beginning.

   b. Many scientists believe that, during microwave experiments, we can actually "hear" echoes of the big bang.

   c. The popular notion is that the big bang was a huge explosion in space, but this is far too simple a description.

   d. The big-bang theory, if accepted, convinces us that the universe was not always as it is now.

20. As the speaker identified various plants found in the fall garden, she selected samples from her display to show her audience the size, shape, texture, and color of each variety.

   a. It will produce red flowers in February—just when gardeners need to see something blooming.

   b. The guest speaker developed a rapport with her audience, and it was evident that she had a great deal of experience and knowledge.

   c. From the most common mums and Montauk daisies to the more exotic euphoria and helenium, she described how gardeners can keep color in their gardens well into November—in sun or in shade.

   d. A list of fall annuals, perennials, and bulbs was available for all participants at the conclusion of the presentation.

21. The reintroduced wolves are producing more offspring than expected.
   a. Ranchers and some biologists are protesting the reintroduction of the wolves.
   b. The gray wolf will be taken off the list of endangered species in the northern Rocky Mountains when ten breeding pairs reside in a region for three years.
   c. There are active efforts to reintroduce wolves to national parks in the United States.
   d. The success of an attempt to reintroduce red wolves to parts of North Carolina is not yet clear.

22. The Puritans established a wide variety of punishments to enforce their strict laws.
   a. The Puritans believed that some lawbreakers should be shamed in public by the use of stocks and the pillory.
   b. Disobedient children would feel the sting of the whip.
   c. The Eighth Amendment of the Bill of Rights prohibits cruel and unusual punishment.
   d. Today, many of the punishments used by the Puritans in Massachusetts Bay seem cruel and excessive.

23. Irish Catholics continued to fight against British rule.
   a. The struggle today is over the control of these six counties.
   b. For centuries, all of Ireland was ruled by Great Britain.
   c. Six counties in the north—where Protestants outnumber Catholics two to one—remained a part of Great Britain and became known as Northern Ireland.
   d. Political violence has claimed many lives in Northern Ireland.

24. In Oklahoma, a girl is forbidden to take a bite from her date's hamburger.
   a. It is illegal for teenagers to take a bath during the winter in Clinton, Indiana.
   b. On Sunday, children may not spin yo-yos in Memphis, Tennessee.
   c. It may be hard to believe, but these strange laws are still on the books!
   d. It is illegal to parade an elephant down Main Street in Austin, Texas.

25. The hairs themselves are very sensitive.
   a. A cat's whiskers are among the most perfect organs of touch.
   b. The roots are provided with highly sensitive nerve endings.
   c. Serving as feelers, they aid the cat's ability to move in the dark.
   d. This is most important for a cat that does its prowling at night.

26. French explorers probably taught the Inuit Eskimos how to play dominoes.
   a. It was known in 181 A.D. in China.
   b. Also, it was played during the 1700s in Italy.
   c. The game of dominoes has been popular for centuries.
   d. From Italy, it was introduced to the rest of the world.

27. It is a fact that people are now living longer than ever before for many reasons.
    a. Some people in the Russia's Caucasus Mountains live to be over one hundred years of age.
    b. No one seems to understand this phenomenon.
    c. Advances in medical science have done wonders for longevity.
    d. The people in this region do not seem to gain anything from medical science.

28. For sixteen years, he spread violence and death throughout the west.
    a. Jesse was gunned down on April 3, 1882.
    b. He left a trail of train and bank robberies.
    c. His crimes were committed during the late 1860s.
    d. Jesse Woodson James was the most legendary of all American outlaws.

Read the following questions that ask you to differentiate fact from opinion. Mark F on your answer sheet if the statement is a fact and O if it is an opinion.

29. Mr. Orenstein is a terrific boss.

30. Many companies have dress-down days on Fridays.

31. Dress-down days improve employee morale.

32. Wednesday is the fourth day of the week.

33. Wednesday is the longest day of the week.

34. There are many different ways to invest your money to provide for a financially secure future.

35. Many people invest in stocks and bonds.

36. Savings accounts and CDs (certificates of deposit) are the best way to invest your hard-earned money.

37. Stocks and bonds are often risky investments.

38. Savings accounts and CDs are fully insured and provide steady, secure interest on your money.

Read the following paragraphs and respond to the questions that ask you to make inferences.

The use of desktop computer equipment and software to create high quality printing for newsletters, business cards, letterhead, and brochures is called Desktop Publishing, or DTP. The most important part of any DTP project is planning. Before you begin, you should know your intended audience, the message you want to communicate, and what form your message will take.

39. This paragraph best supports the statement that
   a. DTP is one way to become acquainted with a new business audience.
   b. computer software is continually being refined to produce more high quality printing.
   c. the first stage of any proposed DTP project should be organization and design.
   d. the planning stage of any DTP project should include talking with the intended audience.

Many office professionals have expressed an interest in replacing the currently used keyboard, known as the QWERTY keyboard, with a keyboard that can keep up with technological changes and make offices more efficient. The best choice is the Dvorak keyboard. Studies have shown that people using the Dvorak keyboard can type 20–30% faster and are able to cut their error rate in half. Dvorak puts vowels and other frequently used letters right under the fingers—on the home row—where typists make 70% of their keystrokes.

40. This paragraph best supports the statement that the Dvorak keyboard
   a. is more efficient than the QWERTY.
   b. has more keys right under the typists' fingers than the QWERTY.
   c. is favored by more typists than the QWERTY.
   d. is—on average— 70% faster than the QWERTY.

Every year Americans use over one billion sharp objects to administer health care in their homes. These sharp objects include lancets, needles, and syringes. If not disposed of in puncture-resistant containers, they can injure sanitation workers. Sharp objects should be disposed of in hard plastic or metal containers with secure lids. The containers should be clearly marked and should be puncture resistant.

41. This paragraph best supports the idea that sanitation workers can be injured if they
   a. do not place sharp objects in puncture-resistant containers.
   b. come in contact with sharp objects that have not been placed in secure containers.
   c. are careless with sharp objects such as lancets, needles, and syringes in their homes.
   d. do not mark the containers they pick up with a warning that those containers contain sharp objects.

One of the missions of the Peace Corps is to bring trained men and women to work in countries who need trained professionals in certain fields. People who work for the Peace Corps are volunteers. However, in order to keep the Peace Corps dynamic and vital, no staff member can work for the agency for more than five years.

42. This paragraph best supports the statement that Peace Corps employees
   a. are highly intelligent people.
   b. must train for about five years.
   c. are hired for a limited term of employment.
   d. have both academic and work experience.

More and more office workers telecommute from offices in their own homes. The benefits of telecommuting allow for greater productivity and greater flexibility. Telecommuters produce an average of 20% more than if they were to work in an office. In addition, their flexible schedule allows them to balance their families with their work responsibilities.

43. This paragraph best supports the statement that telecommuters
   a. get more work done in a given time period than workers who travel to the office.
   b. produce a better quality work product than workers who travel to the office.
   c. are more flexible in their ideas than workers who travel to the office.
   d. would do 20% more work if they were to work in an office.

Close-up images of Mars by the Mariner 9 probe indicated networks of valleys that looked like the stream beds on Earth. These images also implied that Mars once had an atmosphere that was thick enough to trap the sun's heat. If this is true, something must have happened to Mars billions of years ago that stripped away the planet's atmosphere.

44. This paragraph best supports the statement that
   a. Mars once had a thicker atmosphere than Earth does.
   b. the Mariner 9 probe took the first pictures of Mars.
   c. Mars now has little or no atmosphere.
   d. Mars is closer to the sun than Earth is.

It is a myth that labor shortages today center mostly on computer jobs. Although it is true that the lack of computer-related skills accounts for many of the problems in today's job market, there is a lack of skilled labor in many other fields. There is a shortage of uniformed police officers in many cities and a shortage of trained criminal investigators in some rural areas. These jobs may utilize computer skills, but they are not essentially computer jobs.

45. This paragraph best supports the statement that
   a. people with computer skills are in demand in police and criminal investigator jobs.
   b. unemployment in computer-related fields is not as widespread as some people think.
   c. there is a shortage of skilled workers in a variety of fields, including police work.
   d. trained criminal investigators are often underpaid in rural areas.

The competitive civil service system is designed to give candidates fair and equal treatment and to ensure that federal applicants are hired based on objective criteria. Hiring has to be based solely on a candidate's knowledge, skills, and abilities—sometimes abbreviated as *ksa*—and not on external factors such as race, religion, or sex. Whereas employers in the private sector can hire employees for more subjective reasons, federal employers must be able to justify their decision with objective evidence of candidate qualification.

46. This paragraph best supports the statement that
   a. hiring in the private sector is inherently unfair.
   b. *ksa* is not as important as test scores to federal employers.
   c. federal hiring practices are simpler than those employed by the private sector.
   d. the civil service strives to hire on the basis of a candidate's abilities.

It is well known that the world urgently needs adequate distribution of food, but adequate distribution of medicine is just as urgent. Medical expertise and medical supplies need to be redistributed throughout the world so that people in emerging nations will have proper medical care.

47. This paragraph best supports the statement that
   a. the majority of the people in the world have no medical care.
   b. medical resources in emerging nations have diminished in the past few years.
   c. not enough doctors give time and money to those in need of medical care.
   d. many people who live in emerging nations are not receiving proper medical care.

In the past, suggesting a gas tax has usually been considered a political blunder, but that does not seem to be the case today. Several states are promoting bills in their state legislatures that would cut income or property taxes and make up the revenue with taxes on fossil fuel.

48. This paragraph best supports the statement that
   a. gas taxes produce more revenue than income taxes.
   b. states with low income tax rates are increasing their gas taxes.
   c. state legislators no longer fear increasing gas taxes.
   d. taxes on fossil fuels are more popular than property taxes.

Whether you can accomplish a specific goal or meet a specific deadline depends first on how much time you need to get the job done. What should you do when the demands of the job exceed the time you have available? The best approach is to divide the project into smaller pieces. Different goals will have to be divided in different ways, but one seemingly unrealistic goal can often be accomplished by working on several smaller, more reasonable goals.

49. This paragraph best supports the statement that
   a. jobs often remain only partially completed because of lack of time.
   b. the best way to complete projects is to make sure your goals are achievable.
   c. the best way to tackle large projects is to problem-solve first.
   d. the best approach to a demanding job is to delegate responsibility.

Before you begin to compose a business letter, sit down and think about your purpose for writing the letter. Do you want to request information, order a product, register a complaint, or apply for something? Do some brainstorming and gather information before you begin writing. Always keep your objective in mind.

50. This paragraph best supports the statement that
   a. for many different kinds of writing tasks, planning is an important first step.
   b. business letters are frequently complaint letters.
   c. brainstorming and writing take approximately equal amounts of time.
   d. while some people plan ahead when they are writing a business letter, others do not.

ANSWERS

1. d. By stating that fitness walking does not require a commute to a health club, the author stresses the convenience of this form of exercise. The paragraph also states that fitness walking will result in a good workout. Choice **a** is incorrect because no comparison to weight lifting is made. Choice **b** may seem like a logical answer, but the paragraph refers only to people who are fitness walkers, so for others, a health club might be a good investment. Choice **c** is not supported by the passage.

2. d. This answer is implied by the whole paragraph. The author stresses the need to read critically by performing thoughtful and careful operations on the text. Choice **a** is incorrect because the author never says that reading is dull. Choices **b** and **c** are not supported by the paragraph.

3. b. The last sentence in the paragraph clearly gives support for the idea that the interest in Shakespeare is due to the development of his characters. Choice **a** is incorrect because the writer never makes this type of comparison. Choice **c** is wrong because even though scholars are mentioned in the paragraph, there is no indication that the scholars are compiling the anthology. Choice **d** is wrong because there is no support to show that most New Yorkers are interested in this work.

4. a. The support for this choice is in the second sentence, which states that in some countries toxic insecticides are still legal. Choice **b** is incorrect because even though polar regions are mentioned in the paragraph, there is no support for the idea that warmer regions are not just as affected. There is no support for choice **c**. Choice **d** can be ruled out because there is nothing to indicate that DDT and toxaphene are the most toxic.

5. a. The second and third sentence combine to give support to choice **a**. The statement stresses that there must be a judge's approval (i.e., legal authorization) before a search can be conducted. Choices **b** and **d** are incorrect because it is not enough for the police to have direct evidence or a reasonable belief—a judge must authorize the search for it to be legal. Choice **c** is not mentioned in the passage.

6. b. This answer is clearly stated in the last sentence of the paragraph. Choice **a** can be ruled out because there is no support to show that studying math is dangerous. Choice **d** is a contradiction to the information in the passage. There is no support for choice **c**.

7. d. The last sentence states that new technologies are reported daily, and this implies that new technologies are being constantly developed. There is no support for choice **a**. With regard to choice **b**, stone tools were first used two and a half million years ago, but they were not necessarily in use all that time. Choice **c** is clearly wrong because the paragraph states when stone tools first came into use.

8. b. See the second and third sentences for the steps in making ratatouille. Only choice **b** reflects the correct order.

9. d. The main part of the passage describes how to cook vegetables. Only choice **d** indicates that vegetables are included in the dish. The other choices are not reflected in the passage.

10. d. The passage mentions nothing about main or secondary roads.

11. a. The other choices may be true but are not mentioned in the passage.

12. c. The directions indicate that the city prefers, but does not require, the use of the new containers. Also, customers may use more than one container if they purchase an additional one.

13. b. The directions state use of the new containers will expedite pick-up of recyclables. This indicates that the new containers will make the recycling program more efficient.

14. d. The mention that searching for spices has changed the course of history and that nations have gone to war over this condiment implies that the subject of the paragraph is history, not cooking, choices **a**, **b**, and **c**. The use of the word *war* involves danger and intrigue

15. c. The mention of the amazing things the brain is capable of doing is directly relevant to its mysterious and complex nature. Choices **a**, **b**, and **d** are less relevant and specific.

16. b. Choice **b** addresses both of Gary's vanities: his person and his situation. Choice **a** deals only with Gary's vanity of person. Choice **c** deals only with his vanity of position. Choice **d** is not supported in the passage.

17. a. This choice refers both to age and complexity; choices **b** and **c** refer only to complexity. Choice **d** is less relevant to the topic sentence than the other choices.

18. d. Choice **d** reveals the fascination fans had with Marilyn. Choices **a**, **b**, and **c** are merely facts about Marilyn and are not about people's fascination with her.

19. c. The topic sentence speaks of the big-bang theory being much misunderstood, and choice **c** addresses this. The other choices are off topic.

20. c. There are words in this sentence that can be linked to the topic sentence, e.g. fall gardens and the garden in November. In addition, choice **c** lists the different types of flowers the speaker identifies in the topic sentence. Choice **a** speaks of a red flower—unknown to the reader at this point—that blooms in winter, not fall. Choices **b** and **d** give details about the speaker and available hand-outs, but are unrelated to the content of the topic sentence.

21. b. Because the wolves have produced more offspring than expected, chances are they will be taken off the endangered species list. Choices **a**, **c**, and **d** do not reinforce the context of the topic sentence.

22. d. The topic sentence refers to punishment used in early America. Choice **a** gives a reason for the use of punishment in early America. Choices **b** and **c** state why we do not have such punishment today and compares historical punishment with today's sensibility.

23. d. The topic sentence states that violence has claimed many lives in Northern Ireland. Choices **a**, **b**, and **c** only show what led to the situation.

24. c. This choice introduces the idea that some laws are strange. Choices **a**, **b**, and **d** are examples of strange laws, but not the topic sentence.

25. a. This topic sentence states the importance of a cat's whiskers. Choices **b**, **c**, and **d** give other details that do not directly support the topic sentence.

26. c. This choice states the popularity of the game. Choices **a** and **b** state the game's origin. Choice **d** explains how its popularity spread.

27. c. This sentence gives a reason for longevity that was introduced in the topic sentence. Choices **a**, **b**, and **d** are about longevity but do not give any reason.

28. a. Choice **a** pronounces an end to 16 years of violence. Choices **b**, **c**, and **d** are facts about James' life.

29. O. This sentence is an opinion because it can be debated. Someone could just as easily take the opposite position.

30. F. This sentence is a fact. Many companies offer this option.

31. O. This sentence is an opinion. While it could be a good idea, there are no statistics to prove this.

32. F. This sentence is a fact. Wednesday is the fourth day of the week.

33. O. This sentence is an opinion. While Wednesday may seem longer to some people, it is the same length as any other day of the week.

34. F. This sentence is a fact. There are many opportunities for investment.

35. F. This sentence is a fact. People do invest in stocks and bonds.

36. O. This sentence is an opinion. Savings accounts and CDs do not always earn the highest interest rates.

37. F. This sentence is a fact. The stock market can be uncertain.

38. F. This sentence is a fact. Steady, secure interest can be earned using these methods of investing.

39. c. This sentence indicates the importance of organization and design. Choices **a**, **b**, and **d**, even if true, are not in the passage.

40. a. Choice **a** reflects the idea that the Dvorak keyboard is more efficient than the QWERTY. Choices **b**, **c**, and **d** are not in the passage.

41. b. Choice **b** is the only choice that tells how people should dispose of sharp objects in order to avoid placing sanitation workers in danger. Choices **a**, **c**, and **d** discuss how sanitation workers should deal with sharp objects.

42. c. The last sentence of the passage supports choice **c**. Choices **a**, **b**, and **d** are not in the passage.

43. a. Choice **a** details the greater productivity of telecommuters. Choices **b**, **c**, and **d** contain words and phrases from the paragraph, but are incorrect.

44. c. Choice **c** indicates that the atmosphere of Mars has been stripped away.

45. c. Choice **c** expresses the overall theme of the paragraph—a shortage of skilled workers in many fields.

46. d. Choice **d** is the best comprehensive statement about the paragraph.

47. d. Choice **d** is implied by the statement that redistribution is needed so that people in emerging nations can have proper medical care. Choices **a**, **b**, and **c** are not mentioned in the paragraph.

48. c. Choice **c** is supported as the best answer because the paragraph indicates that legislators once feared suggesting gas taxes, but now many of them are promoting bills in favor of these taxes. There is no indication that choice **a** is true. Choice **b** is incorrect because the paragraph does not say why more gas taxes are being proposed. There is no support for choice **d.**

49. c. Choice **c** projects a way to accomplish tasks—by problem-solving, which is the topic of the paragraph.

50. a. Choice **a** is the best overall statement to summarize the message given by the content in the paragraph. Choices **b**, **c**, and **d** do not support the main idea of the paragraph.

CHAPTER

6 Grammar

The ability to write correctly is fundamental for any Civil Service position. This chapter reviews such grammar essentials as sentence boundaries, capitalization, punctuation, subject-verb agreement, verb tenses, pronouns, and commonly confused words.

There is plenty of writing involved in most Civil Service jobs. Forms, memos, e-mails, letters, and reports have to be written during the course of every workday, and the grammar section of the written exam helps the government determine whether an applicant has the competence it takes to complete such tasks. As you apply the vocabulary you have learned in this book, it is important to use these words correctly in sentences. Poor usage can get in the way of what you want to say. Correct usage of standard English shows that you have made the effort to understand the conventions of the English language. When English is used according to the conventions that have been established, your words allow the reader—and your employer or supervisor—to understand exactly what you intend to say. Studying the proper ways to use the vocabulary of the English language can give you a good score on the grammar section of the exam and will show that you are indeed capable and proficient as a writer. The tips and exercises in this chapter will help you ensure that you are ready to excel on this portion of the exam.

▶ COMPLETE SENTENCES AND SENTENCE FRAGMENTS

Sentences are the basic units of written language. Complete sentences express a whole thought. They do not leave you guessing about what the subject is, or what action the subject is taking. When you are writing in the workplace, complete sentences are the correct and accepted format for most pieces of information. For that reason, it is important to distinguish between complete sentences and sentence fragments.

A sentence expresses a complete thought, while a fragment is missing something—it could be a verb or it could be a subject, but the sentence does not express a complete thought. Look at the following examples.

FRAGMENT	COMPLETE SENTENCE
The assistant filing folders.	The assistant was filing folders.
Leaving messages for me.	Janet was always leaving messages for me.

The first fragment in this pair of sentences is an example of a sentence that is missing part of its verb. It needs the helping verb *was* before *filing* to make a complete thought. The second fragment has neither a subject nor a verb. Only when a subject and verb are added is this sentence complete.

Practice
Choose the complete sentence from each pair in the list below.

1. a. We saw the tornado approaching.
   b. When we saw the tornado approaching.

2. a. Before the new house was built in 1972.
   b. The new house was built in 1972.

3. a. Since we are leaving in the morning.
   b. We are leaving in the morning.

Answers
1. a.
2. b.
3. b.

You may have noticed that the choices in each of the questions above are almost the same, but the fragments have an extra word at the beginning. These words are called subordinating conjunctions. When a group of words that would normally be a complete sentence is preceded by a subordinating conjunction, something more is needed to complete the thought. These sentence fragments can easily be corrected:

▶ When we saw the tornado approaching, we headed for cover.

▶ Before the new house was built in 1972, the old house was demolished.

▶ Since we were leaving in the morning, we went to bed early.

Knowing that a subordinating conjunction can signal a sentence fragment, it is a good idea to be familiar with some of the most frequently used subordinating conjunctions. Then you can double-check your work for errors. Use this list as a handy reminder.

after	once	until
although	since	when
as	than	whenever
because	that	where
before	though	wherever
if	unless	while

Run-On Sentences

Run-on sentences are two or more independent clauses (complete sentences) written as though they were one sentence. The main cause of run-on sentences is often faulty punctuation, such as a comma instead of a period between two independent clauses (complete thoughts). End marks like periods, exclamation points, and question marks can solve the run-on sentence problem. Look at the example below.

A complete report had to be submitted every week, it was due on Friday.

This run-on sentence could be corrected in five ways. One way is to add a conjunction after the comma and in-between the two independent clauses. Words such as *and, or, but, as,* or *because* are conjunctions that join sentences.

1. Using the same sentence as a model, it would be considered correct if you wrote:

A complete report had to be submitted every week, and it was due on Friday.

2. It would also be correct to delete the comma and separate the two sentences with a semicolon. A semicolon indicates that the next part of the sentence is a complete sentence, but it is so closely related to the first that there is no reason to make it into a sentence of its own. So, it would be correct to say:

A complete report had to be submitted every week; it was due on Friday.

3. The sentence would be correct if you separated the two independent clauses to make two complete sentences. You could rewrite it as follows:

A complete report had to be submitted every week. It was due on Friday.

4. Adding the subordinating conjunction *because* can fix this sentence as well. It would be correct to say:

A complete report had to be submitted every week because it was due on Friday.

5. Last, the sentence would be correct if written with a dash:

A complete report had to be submitted every week—it was due on Friday.

Practice

Each of the sentences below is a run-on. Correct them on the lines provided using one of the methods listed above.

1. We attended the meeting, we formed some committees.
   Correction: _____

2. Without exception, all of the employees went to lunch at 12:00 they returned at 1:00.
   Correction: _____

3. The defense needed time to examine the new evidence, the lawyer asked for an extension.
   Correction: _____

Answers

1. We attended the meeting, and we formed some committees. OR
   We attended the meeting; we formed some committees.
2. Without exception, all of the employees went to lunch at 12:00, and they returned at 1:00. OR
   Without exception, all of the employees went to lunch at 12:00; they returned at 1:00.
3. The defense needed time to examine the new evidence, and the lawyer asked for an extension.
   OR The defense needed time to examine the new evidence; the lawyer asked for an extension.

Since complete sentences, sentence fragments, and run-on sentences are often grouped together in the grammar section of a test, you may be asked questions like the following on your exam.

Practice

1. Choose the complete sentence.
   a. The books stacked on the floor beside the desk.
   b. After we spent considerable time examining all of the possibilities before making a decision.
   c. In addition to the methods the doctor used to diagnose the problem.
   d. The clues discovered by the archeologists gave us the indication that the historical account of the incident was correct.

2. Choose the complete sentence.
   a. Friday was the best day.
   b. We looking.
   c. Before the door opened.
   d. If we ever see you again.

3. Choose the run-on sentence.
   a. We can fix the printer, or we can buy a new one.
   b. The special services unit completed its work and made its report to the chief.
   c. Unless we hear from the directors of the board before the next meeting, we will not act on the new proposal.
   d. We slept soundly we never heard the alarm.

Answers

   1. d.
   2. a.
   3. d.

▶ CAPITALIZATION

You may encounter questions on your exam that test your ability to use capital letters correctly. If you know the most common capitalization rules, you will be better prepared to correct these errors.

▶ Capitalize the first word of a sentence. If the first word is a number, write it as a word.
▶ Capitalize the pronoun *I*.
▶ Capitalize the first word of a quotation: *"What is the address?" she asked.* Do not capitalize the first word of a partial quotation: *He called me "the best employee" and nominated me for an award.*
▶ Capitalize proper nouns and proper adjectives. Proper nouns are names of people, places, or things, like *Lyndon B. Johnson*; *Austin, Texas*; or *Mississippi River*. They are different from common nouns like *president, city, state,* or *river*. Proper adjectives are adjectives formed from proper nouns. For instance, if the proper noun is *Japan*, the proper adjective would be

Japanese language. If the proper noun is *South America*, the proper adjective would be *South American climate*. See the table that follows for examples of proper nouns and adjectives.

CAPITALIZATION	
Category	**Example of Proper Nouns**
Days of the week	Friday, Saturday
Months of the year	January, February
Holidays	Christmas, Halloween
Special events	Two Rivers Festival, Writers' Conference
Names of individuals	John Henry, George Washington
Names of structures	Lincoln Memorial
Buildings	Empire State Building
Names of trains	Orient Express
Ships	Queen Elizabeth II
Aircraft	Cessna
Product names	Honda Accord
Geographic locations (cities, states, counties, countries, and geographic regions)	Des Moines, Iowa Canada Middle East
Streets	Grand Avenue
Highways	Interstate 29
Roads	Dogwood Road
Landmarks	Continental Divide
Public areas	Grand Canyon, Glacier National Park
Bodies of water	Atlantic Ocean, Mississippi River
Ethnic groups	Asian-American
Languages	English
Nationalities	Irish

Official titles (capitalized only when they appear before a person's name—*Marie Hanson, president of the City Council*, vs. *City Council President Marie Hanson*)	Mayor Bloomberg President Johnson
Institutions	Dartmouth College
Organizations	Girl Scouts
Businesses	Chrysler Corporation
Proper adjectives (a proper adjective is an adjective formed from a proper noun)	English muffins, French cuisine

Practice

The following excerpt contains no capitalized words. Choose those letters that should be capitalized.

> i had just spent a chilly new year's day in sioux falls, south dakota and was driving west toward my home in denver, colorado. it was january 2, 1995. as i traveled along interstate 90, i could see the black hills rising slightly in the distance, and i was shocked by their beauty. president calvin coolidge had called them "a wondrous sight to behold." i now understood why. mount rushmore dominated the landscape. spearfish canyon, a geologic wonder, was full of ponderosa pines and added some greenery to the countryside. nearby, in custer state park, the largest buffalo herd in north america roamed the badlands. fortunately, my jeep cherokee had no trouble with the ice and snow that cold winter day.

Answer

Check your answers against the corrected version:

> I had just spent a chilly New Year's Day in Sioux Falls, South Dakota and was driving west toward my home in Denver, Colorado. It was January 2, 1995. As I traveled along Interstate 90, I could see the Black Hills rising slightly in the distance, and I was shocked by their beauty. President Calvin Coolidge had called them "a wondrous sight to behold." I now understood why. Mount Rushmore dominated the landscape. Spearfish Canyon, a geologic wonder, was full of Ponderosa pines and added some greenery to the countryside. Nearby, in Custer State Park, the largest buffalo herd in North America roamed the Badlands. Fortunately, my Jeep Cherokee had no trouble with the ice and snow that cold winter day.

More Capitalization Practice

Choose the sentence that is capitalized correctly.

1. **a.** This year we will celebrate christmas on Tuesday, December 25 in Manchester, Ohio.
   b. This year we will celebrate Christmas on Tuesday, December 25 in manchester, Ohio.
   c. This year we will celebrate Christmas on Tuesday, December 25 in Manchester, Ohio.
   d. This year we will celebrate christmas on Tuesday, December 25 in manchester, Ohio.

2. **a.** Abraham Adams made an appointment with Mayor Burns to discuss the building plans.
   b. Abraham Adams made an appointment with Mayor Burns to discuss the Building Plans.
   c. Abraham Adams made an appointment with mayor Burns to discuss the Building plans.
   d. Abraham Adams made an appointment with mayor Burns to discuss the Building Plans.

3. **a.** Ms. Abigail Dornburg, M.D., was named head of the review board for Physicians Mutual.
   b. Ms. Abigail Dornburg, M.D., was named Head of the Review Board for Physicians Mutual.
   c. Ms. Abigail Dornburg, m.d. Was named head of the review board for Physicians mutual.
   d. Ms. Abigail dornburg, M.D., was named head of the review board for Physicians Mutual.

Answers
1. **c.**
2. **a.**
3. **a.** Note: The words "review board" are common nouns and not the specific title of a particular committee or panel. There is no need to capitalize them in this sentence.

▶ PUNCTUATION

A section on the written exam may test your punctuation skills. Knowing how to use periods, commas, and apostrophes correctly will effectively boost your score on the exam.

Periods

If you know the most common rules for using periods, you will have a much easier time spotting and correcting sentence errors.

- ▶ Use a period at the end of a sentence that is not a question or an exclamation.
- ▶ Use a period after an initial in a name.
  Example: John F. Kennedy
- ▶ Use a period after an abbreviation, unless the abbreviation is an acronym.
  Abbreviations: Mr., Ms., Dr., A.M., General Motors Corp., Allied, Inc.
  Acronyms: NASA, SCUBA, RADAR
- ▶ If a sentence ends with an abbreviation, use only one period.
  Example: We brought pens, paper, pencils, etc.

Commas

Commas are more important than many people realize. The correct use of commas helps present ideas and information clearly to readers. Missing or misplaced commas, on the other hand, can confuse readers and convey a message quite different from what was intended. This chart demonstrates just how much impact commas can have on meaning.

There is an indeterminate number of people in this sentence.	My sister Diane John Carey Melissa and I went to dinner.
There are four people in this sentence.	My sister Diane, John Carey, Melissa, and I went to dinner.
There are five people in this sentence.	My sister, Diane, John Carey, Melissa, and I went to dinner.
There are six people in this sentence.	My sister, Diane, John, Carey, Melissa, and I went to dinner.

If you know the most common rules for using commas, you will have a much easier time identifying sentence errors and correcting them.

▶ Use a comma before *and, but, so, or, for, nor,* and *yet* when they separate two groups of words that could be complete sentences.
Example: The manual listed the steps in sequence, and that made it easy for any reader to follow.
▶ Use a comma to separate items in a series.
Example: The student driver stopped, looked, and listened when she approached the railroad tracks.

You may wonder if the comma after the last item in a series is really necessary. This is called a serial comma, and is used to ensure clarity.

▶ Use a comma to separate two or more adjectives modifying the same noun.
Example: The hot, black, rich coffee was just what I needed on Monday morning. (Notice that there is no comma between *rich*—an adjective—and *coffee*—the noun it describes.)
▶ Use a comma after introductory words, phrases, or clauses in a sentence.
Example of an introductory word: Usually, the secretary reads the minutes of the meeting. Example of an introductory phrase: During her lunch break, she went shopping. Example of an introductory clause: After we found the source of the problem, it was easily rectified.
▶ Use a comma after a name followed by Jr., Sr., M.D., Ph.D., or any other abbreviation.
Example: The ceremony commemorated Martin Luther King, Jr. Remember that commas should be on both sides of an abbreviation—*The life of Martin Luther King, Jr., was the subject of the documentary.*
▶ Use a comma to separate items in an address.
Example: The package was addressed to 1433 West G Avenue, Orlando, Florida, 36890.
▶ Use a comma to separate a day and a year, as well as after the year when it is in a sentence.
Example: I was born on July 21, 1954, during a thunderstorm.

▶ Use a comma after the greeting of a friendly letter and after the closing of a letter.
   Example of a greeting: Dear Uncle John,
   Example of a closing: Sincerely yours,
▶ Use a comma to separate contrasting elements in a sentence.
   Example: Your speech needs strong arguments, not strong opinions, to convince me.
▶ Use commas to set off appositives—words or phrases that explain or identify the noun in a sentence.
   Example: My dog, a dachshund, is named Penny.

Practice

The following paragraph contains no commas or periods. Add commas and periods as needed.

Dr Newton Brown Jr a renowned chemist has held research positions for OPEC Phillips Petroleum Inc Edward L Smith Chemical Designs and R J Reynolds Co His thorough exhaustive research is recognized in academic circles as well as in the business community as the most well-designed reliable data available Unfortunately on July 6 1988 he retired after a brief but serious illness He lives in a secluded retirement community at 2401 Beach Drive Sarasota Springs Florida

Answer

Check your version against the following corrected paragraph.

Dr. Newton Brown, Jr., a renowned chemist, has held research positions for OPEC, Phillips Petroleum Inc., Edward L. Smith Chemical Designs, and R. J. Reynolds Co. His thorough, exhaustive research is recognized in academic circles, as well as in the business community, as the most well-designed, reliable data available. Unfortunately, on July 6, 1988, he retired after a brief but serious illness. He lives in a secluded retirement community at 2401 Beach Drive, Sarasota Springs, Florida.

Apostrophes

Apostrophes are used to show ownership or relationships, to show where letters have been omitted in a contraction, and to form the plurals of numbers and letters.

If you know the most common rules for using apostrophes, you will have a much easier time spotting and correcting punctuation errors.

▶ Use an apostrophe in contractions. This tells the reader that a letter has been omitted.
Examples: do not = don't
   I will = I'll
   it is = it's
▶ Use an apostrophe to form the plural of numbers and letters.
Examples: There are two o's and two m's in the word roommate.
   She chose four a's on the multiple choice exam.
▶ Use an apostrophe to show possession.

USING APOSTROPHES TO SHOW POSSESSION		
Singular Nouns **Rule: add 's**	**Plural Nouns ending in *s*** **Rule: add '**	**Plural nouns not ending in *s*** **Rule: add 's**
boy's	boys'	men's
child's	kids'	children's
lady's	ladies'	women's

Since apostrophes, commas, and periods are often grouped together in the grammar section of a test, you may be asked questions like the following on your exam.

Practice

Choose the sentence that is punctuated correctly.

1. **a.** The reviewers purpose for interviewing Dr. E. S. Sanders Jr. was to gather more information to include in the newspaper article.

    b. The reviewer's purpose for interviewing Dr. E. S. Sanders, Jr. was to gather more information to include in the newspaper article.

    c. The reviewer's purpose for interviewing Dr. E. S. sanders, Jr., was to gather more information to include in the newspaper article.

    d. The reviewer's purpose for interviewing Dr. E. S. Sanders, Jr. was to gather more information, to include in the newspaper article.

2. **a.** During the town board meeting Mr. Peterson volunteered to make a detailed list of community members who would help pick up litter, set up picnic tables, and distribute flyers for the opening of the town beach on May 31, 2003.

    b. During the town board meeting, Mr. Peterson volunteered to make a detailed list of community members who would help pick up litter set up picnic tables, and distribute flyers for the opening of the town beach on May 31 2003.

    c. During the town board meeting, Mr. Peterson volunteered to make a detailed list of community members who would help pick up litter set up picnic tables and distribute flyers for the opening of the town beach on May 31 2003.

    d. During the town board meeting, Mr. Peterson volunteered to make a detailed list of community members who would help pick up litter, set up picnic tables, and distribute flyers for the opening of the town beach on May 31, 2003.

3. **a.** When all of the candidates were interviewed, it was determined that four people would be chosen to fill the openings left by this years retirements.

　　b. When all of the candidates were interviewed, it was determined that four people would be chosen to fill the openings left by this year's retirements.

　　c. When all of the candidate's were interviewed it was determined that four people would be chosen to fill the openings left by this year's retirements.

　　d. When all of the candidate's were interviewed, it was determined that four people would be chosen to fill the openings left by this years retirements.

Answers

　1. d.
　2. d.
　3. b.

▶ VERBS

The *subject* of a sentence—who or what the sentence is about, the person or thing performing the action—should agree with its verb in number. Simply put, this means that if a subject is singular, the verb must be singular; if the subject is plural, the verb must be plural. If you are unsure whether a verb is singular or plural, use this simple test. Fill in the blanks below using the verb *speak*. Be sure that it agrees with the subject.

　　He _____. (The correct form of the verb in this sentence would be singular because the subject—*he*—is singular. The sentence, written correctly, would be: He *speaks*.)
　　They _____. (The correct form of the verb in this sentence would be plural because the subject—*they*—is plural. The sentence, written correctly, would be: They *speak*.)

　　Try this simple test with other verbs such as *sing, write, think,* or *plan* if you are confused about subject/verb agreement. Notice that a verb ending with *s* is usually a sign of the singular form of the verb, and there would be a singular subject in the sentence. Similarly, a subject ending with *s* is the sign of a plural subject, and the verb in the sentence would be plural.

　　If a sentence includes a verb phrase (a main verb and one or more helping verbs), the helping verb (a verb that helps the main verb express action or make a statement) has to agree with the subject.

　　Examples: The **gymnast is** performing.
　　　　　　　The **gymnasts are** performing.
　　　　　　　The new **schedule has interfered** with our plans.
　　　　　　　The new **schedules have interfered** with our plans.

Practice

The subjects and verbs in this list are in agreement. Identify the singular subject-verb pairs with an *S* and the plural with a *P*.

_____ **1.** birds fly

_____ **2.** wind howls

_____ **3.** members meet

_____ **4.** Jack knows

_____ **5.** motor runs

Answers
1. P
2. S
3. P
4. S
5. S

Practice

Choose the correct verb for each of the following sentences. Remember that the verbs have to be in agreement with their subjects.

1. The flowers (were/was) arranged carefully.

2. The meeting (starts/start) promptly at 10:00.

3. That decision (changes/change) everything.

4. Computers (saves/save) time.

5. Lightning (strikes/strike) indiscriminately.

Answers
1. were
2. starts
3. changes
4. save
5. strikes

Agreement When Using Pronoun Subjects

Few people have trouble matching noun subjects and verbs, but pronouns are sometimes difficult for even the most sophisticated writers. Some pronouns are always singular; others are always plural. Still others can be either singular or plural, depending on the usage.

These pronouns are always singular:

each	everyone
either	no one
neither	one
anybody	nobody
anyone	someone
everybody	somebody

For example, you would say "Neither of them *has* been to Chicago"—not "Neither of them *have* been to Chicago." *Neither* is the subject, so the verb must be singular.

The indefinite pronouns *each*, *either*, and *neither* are most often misused. You can avoid a mismatch by mentally adding the word *one* after the pronoun and removing the other words between the pronoun and the verb. Look at the following examples.

Each of the men wants his own car.
Each **one** of the men wants his own car.
Either of the sales clerks knows where the sale merchandise is located.
Either **one** of the sales clerks knows where the sale merchandise is located.

It is important to note that a subject is never found in a prepositional phrase. Any noun or pronoun found in a prepositional phrase is the object of the preposition, and this word can never be the subject of the sentence. Try to filter out prepositional phrases when looking for the subject of a sentence. Using the two sentences above as models, note the prepositional phrases in bold. When you have identified these phrases, you will have a much easier time finding the subject of the sentence.

Each **of the men** wants his own car.
Either **of the sales clerks** knows where the sale merchandise is located.

These kinds of sentences may sound awkward because many speakers misuse these pronouns, and you may be used to hearing them used incorrectly. To be sure that you are using them correctly, the substitution trick—inserting *one* for the words following the pronoun—will help you avoid making an error.

Some pronouns are always plural and require a plural verb. They are:

both	many
few	several

Other pronouns can be either singular or plural:

all	none
any	some
most	

The words or prepositional phrases following these pronouns determine whether they are singular or plural. If what follows the pronoun is plural, the verb must be plural. If what follows is singular, the verb must be singular.

All of the **work is** finished.
All of the **jobs are** finished.
Is any of the **pizza** left?
Are any of the **pieces** of pizza left?
None of the **time was** wasted.
None of the **minutes were** wasted.

If two nouns or pronouns are joined by *and*, they require a plural verb.

He **and** she want to buy a new house.
Bill **and** Verna want to buy a new house.

If two nouns or pronouns are joined by *or* or *nor*, they require a singular verb. Think of them as two separate sentences, and you will never make a mistake in agreement.

He **or** she wants to buy a new house.
He wants to buy a new house.
She wants to buy a new house.
Neither Portuguese nor Dutch is widely spoken today.
Portuguese is not widely spoken today.
Dutch is not widely spoken today.

Practice

Choose the correct verb in each of the following sentences. Remember that the subject and verb have to agree in number.

1. Every other day, either Gayle or Diane (takes/take) out the trash.

2. A woman from my neighborhood (works/work) at the Community Theater box office.

3. A good knowledge of the rules (helps/help) you understand the game.

4. Each of these prescriptions (has/have) side effects.

5. Do all of the chapters (describes/describe) a different character?

Answers

1. **takes.** The subject is either [Gayle or Diane] and uses the singular verb *takes*.
2. **works.** The subject is *woman* and takes the singular verb *works*.
3. **helps.** The subject is *knowledge* and takes the singular verb *helps*.
4. **has.** The subject is *each* and takes the singular verb *has*.
5. **describe.** The subject is *all* and takes the plural verb *describe*.

▶ VERB TENSE

The tense of a verb tells the reader when the action occurs, occurred, or will occur. Present tense verbs let the reader imagine the action as it is being read. Past tense verbs tell the reader what has already happened. Future tense verbs tell the reader what will happen.

Read the three paragraphs that follow. The first is written in the present tense, the second in the past tense, and the third in the future tense. Notice the difference in the verbs; they are highlighted so that you can easily see them.

1. To plan for growth in the small city, a city planner **is hired** to speak to the town council. The city planner **presents** a map of the city where some public buildings **are located**. Each of the squares on the map **represents** one city block. Street names **are labeled**. Arrows on streets **indicate** that the street **is** one way only in the direction of the arrow. Two-way traffic **is** allowed on streets with no arrows. This plan **alleviates** traffic in the downtown area.

2. To plan for growth in the small city, a city planner **was hired**. The city planner **presented** a map of the city where some public buildings **were located**. Each of the squares on the map **represented** one city block. Street names **were labeled**. Arrows on streets **indicated** that the street **was** one way only in the direction of the arrow. Two-way traffic **was** allowed on streets with no arrows. This plan **alleviated** traffic in the downtown area.

3. To plan for growth in the small city, a city planner **will be hired**. The city planner **will present** a map of the city where some public buildings **will be located**. Each of the squares on the map **will represent** one city block. Street names **will be labeled**. Arrows on streets **will indicate**

that the street **will be** one way only in the direction of the arrow. Two-way traffic **will be allowed** on streets with no arrows. This plan **will alleviate** traffic in the downtown area.

It is easy to distinguish present, past, and future tense by trying the word in a sentence beginning with *today* (present tense), *yesterday* (past tense), or *tomorrow* (future tense).

VERB TENSE		
Present Tense	**Past Tense**	**Future Tense**
Today, I _____	Yesterday, I _____	Tomorrow, I _____
drive	drove	will drive
think	thought	will think
rise	rose	will rise
catch	caught	will catch

The important thing to remember about verb tense is to be consistent. If a passage begins in the present tense, keep it in the present tense unless there is a specific reason to change—to indicate that some action occurred in the past, for instance. If a passage begins in the past tense, it should remain in the past tense. Similarly, if a passage begins in the future tense, it should remain in the future tense. Verb tense should never be mixed as it is in the following sample.

Incorrect
The doorman **opens** the door and **saw** the crowd of people.
Correct
Present Tense: The doorman *opens* the door and *sees* the crowd of people.
Past Tense: The doorman *opened* the door and *saw* the crowd of people.
Future Tense: The doorman *will open* the door and *will see* the crowd of people.

Sometimes it is necessary to use a different verb tense in order to clarify when an action took place. Read the following sentences and their explanations.

1. The game warden **sees** the fish that you **caught**. (The verb *sees* is in the present tense and indicates that the action is occurring in the present. The verb *caught* is in the past tense and indicates that the fish were caught at some earlier time.)
2. The house that **was built** over a century ago **sits** on top of the hill. (The verb **was built** is in the past tense and indicates that the house was built in the past. The verb **sits** is in the present tense and indicates that the action is still occurring.)

Practice

Choose the sentence that uses the verb tense correctly.

1. **a.** When I run, I always run fast.
   b. When I run, I always ran fast.
   c. When I ran, I always run fast.
   d. When I ran, I always have ran fast.

2. **a.** Her glasses were broke, and she had trouble reading the manual.
   b. Her glasses were broken, and she had trouble reading the manual.
   c. Her glasses was broke, and she have trouble reading the manual.
   d. Her glasses is broken, and she has trouble reading the manual.

3. **a.** It begin to snow, and the bank closed early.
   b. It beginning to snow, and the bank closed early.
   c. It was begin to snow, and the bank is closed early.
   d. It began to snow, and the bank closed early.

Answers
   1. a.
   2. b.
   3. d.

Pronouns

Using a single pronoun in a sentence is usually easy to do. In fact, most people would readily be able to identify the mistakes in the following sentences.

> **Me** went to the movie with **he**.
> My instructor gave **she** a ride to the class.

Most people know that *Me* in the first sentence should be *I* and that *he* should be *him*. In the second sentence, *she* should be *her*. Such errors are easy to spot when the pronouns are used alone in a sentence. The problem occurs when a pronoun is used with a noun or another pronoun. See if you can spot the errors in the following sentences.

> The director rode with Jerry and **I**.
> Belle and **him** are going to the company picnic.

The errors in these sentences are not as easy to spot as those in the sentences using a single pronoun. In order to remedy this problem, you can turn the sentence with two pronouns into two separate sentences. Then the error becomes more clear.

The director rode with Jerry.

The director rode with **me** (not *I*).

Belle is going to the company picnic.

He (not *him*) is going to the company picnic.

To help you move through this grammar problem with ease, you should know that subject pronouns—those that are the subject in a sentence or the predicate nominative—are in the nominative case. (A predicate nominative is a noun or pronoun that is the same as the subject. For example: It was I. In this sentence, the subject *it* is the same as the pronoun *I*.) Subjective pronouns are *I*, *he*, *she*, *we*, and *they*.

Objective pronouns—those that are the object of a preposition or the direct/indirect object of the sentence—are in the objective case. (A direct object is the word that receives the action of the verb or shows the result of the action. It answers the question *who* or *whom*. For example: She went with *me*. An indirect object is the word that comes before the direct object. It tells *to whom* or *for whom* the action of the verb is done. For example: She gave *me* some flowers on my birthday.)

Objective pronouns are: *me*, *him*, *her*, *us*, and *them*. *You* and *it* do not change their forms, so there is no need to memorize case for those words.

Knowing when to use objective pronouns can become problematic when they are used in compounds such as:

She directed her comments to Margaret and me.

A simple way to find the correct pronoun is to test each one separately.

She directed her comments to Margaret.

She directed her comments to me.

Pronoun Agreement

Using singular and plural pronouns can be a problem at times. Like subjects and verbs, pronouns must match the number of the nouns they represent. If the noun that a pronoun represents is singular, the pronoun must be singular. On the other hand, if the noun a pronoun represents is plural, the pronoun must be plural. Sometimes a pronoun represents another pronoun. If so, either both pronouns must be singular or both pronouns must be plural. Consult the list of singular and plural pronouns you saw earlier in this chapter.

The *doctor* must take a break when *she* is tired. (singular)

Doctors must take breaks when *they* are tired. (plural)

One of the girls misplaced *her* purse. (singular)

All of the girls misplaced *their* purses. (plural)

If two or more singular nouns or pronouns are joined by *and*, use a plural pronoun to represent them.

> If *he and she* want to join us, *they* are welcome to do so.
> *Mark and Jennifer* planned a meeting to discuss *their* ideas.

If two or more singular nouns or pronouns are joined by *or*, use a singular pronoun. If a singular and a plural noun or pronoun are joined by *nor*, the pronoun should agree with the closest noun or pronoun it represents.

> The *bank or the credit union* can lend money to *its* patrons.
> The *treasurer or the assistant* will loan you *his* calculator.
> Neither *the soldiers nor the sergeant* was sure of *his* location.
> Neither *the sergeant nor the soldiers* was sure of *their* location.

Practice

Choose the correct pronoun in the following sentences.

1. Andrew or Alex will bring (his/their) camera so (he/they) can take pictures of the party.

2. One of the file folders is not in (its/their) drawer.

3. The auto parts store sent Bob and Neil the parts (he/they) ordered.

4. Carolyn and (he/him) went to the movies with Lisa and (I/me).

5. Neither my cousins nor my uncle knows what (he/they) will do tomorrow.

Answers

1. his, he
2. its
3. they
4. he, me
5. he

▶ WORDS COMMONLY CONFUSED

The following word pairs are often misused in written language. By reading the explanations below and looking at the examples, you can learn to use these words correctly every time.

Its/It's

Its is a possessive pronoun and shows that something belongs to *it*. *It's* is a contraction for *it is* or *it has*. The only time you should ever use *it's* is when you can also substitute the words *it is* or *it has*.

The dog knows *its* way home.

It's only fair that I should do the dishes for you tonight.

That/Who

That refers to things. *Who* refers to people.

There is the man *who* helped me find my wallet.

The office worker *who* invented Wite-Out® was very creative.

This is the house *that* my sister bought.

The book *that* I need is no longer in print.

There/Their/They're

Their is a possessive pronoun that shows ownership. *There* is an adverb that tells where an action or item is located. *They're* is a contraction for the words *they are*. It is easy to remember the differences if you remember these tips.

▶ *Their* means belonging to them. Of the three words, *their* can be most easily transformed into the word *them*. Extend the *r* on the right side and connect the *i* and the *r* to turn *their* into *them*. This clue will help you remember that *their* means that it belongs to them. *Their* coats should be hanging on racks by the door.

▶ If you examine the word *there*, you can see that it contains the word *here*. Whenever you use *there*, you should be able to substitute *here*, and the sentence should still make sense. She told me to wait over *there* for the next available salesperson.

▶ Imagine that the apostrophe in *they're* is actually a very small letter *a*. Use *they're* in a sentence only when you can substitute *they are*. Yes, *they're* coming to dinner with us next Saturday night.

Your/You're

Your is a possessive pronoun that means something belongs to you. *You're* is a contraction for the words *you are*. The only time you should use *you're* is when you can substitute the words *you are*.

Your name will be the next one called.

You're the next person to be called.

To/Too/Two

To can be used as a preposition or an infinitive.

▶ **A preposition** shows relationships between other words in a sentence.
Example: My car is *in* the employee parking lot.
The word *in* shows the relation of *my car* to the *parking lot*. The meaning of the sentence would be different if another preposition such as *on*, *over*, or *beside* were used. Other examples: *to* the office, *in* the red, *to* my church, *beside* the table, *over* the top, *at* his restaurant, *to* our disadvantage, *in* an open room, *by* the door

▶ An **infinitive** is *to* followed by a verb. For example: *to* talk, *to* deny, *to* see, *to* find, *to* advance, *to* read, *to* build, *to* want, *to* misinterpret, *to* peruse
To find the correct answer, I did some very careful thinking.

Too means *also*. To see if you are using the correct spelling of the word *too*, substitute the word *also*. The sentence should still make sense.

I did not know that you wanted to go *too*.

Too can also mean *excessively*: It was *too* hot inside the car.

Two is a number, as in one, *two*. If you memorize this, you will never misuse this form.

There are only *two* people in our party.

Practice

Choose the correct form of these words commonly confused.

1. (Its/it's) (to/too/two) late (to/too/two) remedy the situation now.

2. Where is the librarian (who/that) helped me with the research material?

3. (There/Their/They're) going (to/too/two) begin construction as soon as the plans are finished.

4. We left (there/their/they're) house after the storm subsided.

5. I think (your/you're) going (to/too/two) win at least (to/too/two) more times.

6. The corporation moved (its/it's) home office.

Answers

1. It's, too, to
2. who
3. They're, to
4. their
5. you're, to, two
6. its

GRAMMAR CHECKLIST

To answer grammar questions on the Civil Service exam, you should be able to

- ✓ identify complete sentences and sentence fragments.
- ✓ check for correct punctuation, such as periods, commas, and apostrophes.
- ✓ look for subject-verb agreement and consistency of verb tense.
- ✓ check pronouns to make sure the correct form is used and that the number (singular or plural) is correct.
- ✓ recognize words commonly confused.

As you answer grammar questions in multiple-choice format,

- ✓ read all of the answer choices before selecting the correct answer.
- ✓ when selecting an answer, do not waste time going back to review answer choices you have already eliminated as being wrong.
- ✓ skip over questions you do not know and come back to them later.
- ✓ leave spaces for those questions you skipped.
- ✓ return to any questions you skipped, read them carefully, and make a choice.
- ✓ check all of your answers, if you have time, at the end of the test.

PRACTICE QUESTIONS

The 50 questions in this exercise test your knowledge of complete sentences/sentence fragments, punctuation, subject-verb agreement, verb tense, pronouns, and words commonly confused.

1.	ⓐ	ⓑ	ⓒ	ⓓ	26.	ⓐ	ⓑ	ⓒ	ⓓ
2.	ⓐ	ⓑ	ⓒ	ⓓ	27.	ⓐ	ⓑ	ⓒ	ⓓ
3.	ⓐ	ⓑ	ⓒ	ⓓ	28.	ⓐ	ⓑ	ⓒ	ⓓ
4.	ⓐ	ⓑ	ⓒ	ⓓ	29.	ⓐ	ⓑ	ⓒ	ⓓ
5.	ⓐ	ⓑ	ⓒ	ⓓ	30.	ⓐ	ⓑ	ⓒ	ⓓ
6.	ⓐ	ⓑ	ⓒ	ⓓ	31.	ⓐ	ⓑ	ⓒ	ⓓ
7.	ⓐ	ⓑ	ⓒ	ⓓ	32.	ⓐ	ⓑ	ⓒ	ⓓ
8.	ⓐ	ⓑ	ⓒ	ⓓ	33.	ⓐ	ⓑ	ⓒ	ⓓ
9.	ⓐ	ⓑ	ⓒ	ⓓ	34.	ⓐ	ⓑ	ⓒ	ⓓ
10.	ⓐ	ⓑ	ⓒ	ⓓ	35.	ⓐ	ⓑ	ⓒ	ⓓ
11.	ⓐ	ⓑ	ⓒ	ⓓ	36.	ⓐ	ⓑ	ⓒ	ⓓ
12.	ⓐ	ⓑ	ⓒ	ⓓ	37.	ⓐ	ⓑ	ⓒ	ⓓ
13.	ⓐ	ⓑ	ⓒ	ⓓ	38.	ⓐ	ⓑ	ⓒ	ⓓ
14.	ⓐ	ⓑ	ⓒ	ⓓ	39.	ⓐ	ⓑ	ⓒ	ⓓ
15.	ⓐ	ⓑ	ⓒ	ⓓ	40.	ⓐ	ⓑ	ⓒ	ⓓ
16.	ⓐ	ⓑ	ⓒ	ⓓ	41.	ⓐ	ⓑ	ⓒ	ⓓ
17.	ⓐ	ⓑ	ⓒ	ⓓ	42.	ⓐ	ⓑ	ⓒ	ⓓ
18.	ⓐ	ⓑ	ⓒ	ⓓ	43.	ⓐ	ⓑ	ⓒ	ⓓ
19.	ⓐ	ⓑ	ⓒ	ⓓ	44.	ⓐ	ⓑ	ⓒ	ⓓ
20.	ⓐ	ⓑ	ⓒ	ⓓ	45.	ⓐ	ⓑ	ⓒ	ⓓ
21.	ⓐ	ⓑ	ⓒ	ⓓ	46.	ⓐ	ⓑ	ⓒ	ⓓ
22.	ⓐ	ⓑ	ⓒ	ⓓ	47.	ⓐ	ⓑ	ⓒ	ⓓ
23.	ⓐ	ⓑ	ⓒ	ⓓ	48.	ⓐ	ⓑ	ⓒ	ⓓ
24.	ⓐ	ⓑ	ⓒ	ⓓ	49.	ⓐ	ⓑ	ⓒ	ⓓ
25.	ⓐ	ⓑ	ⓒ	ⓓ	50.	ⓐ	ⓑ	ⓒ	ⓓ

For questions 1–8, look for run-on sentences or sentence fragments. Choose the answer choice that does NOT express a correct, complete sentence. If there are no mistakes, select choice d.

1. **a.** Manuel wanted to complete all of his courses so he could get his degree.
   b. She couldn't believe the premise of the story.
   c. The train leaving the station.
   d. no mistakes

2. **a.** At the end of the day, they hoped to be finished with all tasks.
   b. When will you teach me how to cook like you do?
   c. I can't wait Janet can't either.
   d. no mistakes

3. **a.** The medieval literature class was very interesting.
   b. The children in the park, including all of the girls on the swings.
   c. Christina is an excellent elementary school teacher.
   d. no mistakes

4. **a.** Sandra Day O'Connor was the first woman to serve on the U.S. Supreme Court.
   b. We visited the presidential library of Lyndon B. Johnson.
   c. I saw Dr. Sultana because Dr. Das was on vacation.
   d. no mistakes

5. **a.** What is the best route to Philadelphia?
   b. The artichokes cost more than the asparagus does.
   c. Turn off the television it's time for dinner!
   d. no mistakes

6. **a.** Baseball is the national pastime of the United States.
   b. Ernest Hemingway won the Nobel Prize for Literature.
   c. The rest of the story coming to you later.
   d. no mistakes

7. **a.** The sky was a brilliant blue this morning.
   b. John is an avid stamp collector.
   c. Elvis Presley's home is in Memphis, Tennessee.
   d. no mistakes

8. **a.** If you see a grizzly bear, do not make any sudden movements.
   b. The county executive a person who works very hard.
   c. The national park system in the United States preserves land for all to enjoy.
   d. no mistakes

For questions 9–13, choose the sentence that uses commas correctly.

9. **a.** Ecstatic the winner hugged her coach.
   b. My best friend, James, is always on time.
   c. As far as I know that room is empty.
   d. Maureen, my cousin is going to Hawaii in August.

10. **a.** Concerned about her health, Jessica made an appointment to see a doctor.
   b. Those sneakers are available in black tan red, and white.
   c. After checking our equipment we began our hiking trip.
   d. Exhausted I climbed into bed.

11. **a.** Hoping for the best, I called Dan.
   b. We visited England, France Spain, and Italy.
   c. You can have chocolate ice cream or you can have a dish of vanilla pudding.
   d. Timothy however will attend a community college in the fall.

12. **a.** Max was the most physically fit and he won the 5K race.
   b. Shortly she will answer all messages.
   c. My physician, Dr. O'Connor, told me I was very healthy.
   d. Bonnie was outgoing friendly and sociable.

13. **a.** After his vacation to the Caribbean Art decided to learn scuba diving.
   b. I like jazz, classical, and blues music.
   c. My good friend, Melanie sent me a picture of her new puppy.
   d. The abundant, blue, violets were scattered everywhere in the woodland garden.

For questions 14–19, choose the sentence or phrase that has a mistake in capitalization or punctuation. If you find no mistakes, select choice d.

14. **a.** My favorite season is Spring.
   b. Last Monday, Aunt Ruth took me shopping.
   c. We elected Ben as treasurer of the freshman class.
   d. no mistakes

15. **a.** He shouted from the window, but we couldn't hear him.
   b. NASA was launching its first space shuttle of the year.
   c. The boys' wore identical sweaters.
   d. no mistakes

16. **a.** Occasionally someone will stop and ask for directions.
   b. When you come to the end of Newton Road, turn left onto Wilson Street.
   c. Lauren's father is an auto mechanic.
   d. no mistakes

17.   **a.** That book must be yours.

      b. This is someone elses coat.

      c. Don B. Norman was one of the founders of the community.

      d. no mistakes

18.   **a.** The US flag should be flown proudly.

      b. She served eggs, toast, and orange juice for breakfast.

      c. He wanted turkey, lettuce, and mayonnaise on his sandwich.

      d. no mistakes

19.   **a.** Dear Anne,

      b. Sincerely, yours

      c. Yours truly,

      d. no mistakes

For questions 20–25, choose the correct verb form.

20. I am trying to become more skilled at weaving before winter _____

      a. arrived.

      b. will have arrived.

      c. will arrive.

      d. arrives.

21. While trying to _____ his cat from a tree, he fell and hurt himself.

      a. be rescuing

      b. have rescued

      c. rescue

      d. rescuing

22. The volunteers from the fire department _____ quickly and extinguished a fire on North Country Road.

      a. will respond

      b. responded

      c. will have responded

      d. have responded

23. In Tuesday's paper, the owner of the supermarket was recognized for helping a customer who _____ on the icy sidewalk.

      a. falls

      b. would fall

      c. had fallen

      d. has fallen

24. The people who bought this old lamp at the antique auction _____ very smart.
    a. was
    b. were
    c. is
    d. has been

25. I _____ her speak on Friday night about the advantages of organic gardening.
    a. will have heard
    b. would hear
    c. would have heard
    d. will hear

For questions 26–30, choose the correct pronoun form.

26. That snappy looking sports car belongs to my sister and _____.
    a. I
    b. me
    c. mine
    d. myself

27. The person _____ made this delicious cheesecake has my vote.
    a. that
    b. which
    c. who
    d. whose

28. George and Michael left _____ backpacks in the car.
    a. his
    b. their
    c. there
    d. its

29. We arranged the flowers and placed _____ in the center of the table.
    a. them
    b. this
    b. it
    b. that

30. _____ met more than ten years ago at a mutual friend's birthday party.
    a. Her and I
    b. Her and me
    c. She and me
    d. She and I

For questions 31–40, find the sentence that has a mistake in grammar or usage. If there are no mistakes, select choice d.

31. **a.** Have you ever read the book called *The Firm*?
   b. She urged me not to go.
   c. Stop, look, and listen.
   d. no mistakes

32. **a.** Three's a crowd.
   b. If you're not sure, look in the dictionary.
   c. They weren't the only ones that didn't like the movie.
   d. no mistakes.

33. **a.** Anne will leave first and Nick will follow her.
   b. Maya Angelou, a famous poet, recently spoke at our school.
   c. The clerk asked for my address and phone number.
   d. no mistakes

34. **a.** That parrot doesnt talk.
   b. Don't spend too much money.
   c. We waited until he stopped to make a phone call.
   d. no mistakes

35. **a.** Alberto laughed loudly when he saw us.
   b. They're looking for another apartment.
   c. The first house on the street is there's.
   d. no mistakes

36. **a.** I love the fireworks on the Fourth of July.
   b. The dog's barking woke us from a sound sleep.
   c. My grandparents live in Dallas, Texas.
   d. no mistakes

37. **a.** Ursula has broke one of your plates.
   b. The sun rose from behind the mountains.
   c. Don't spend too much time on that project.
   d. no mistakes

38. **a.** She believed in keeping a positive attitude.
   b. After we sat down to eat dinner, the phone rung.
   c. Sign all three copies of the form.
   d. no mistakes

39. a. The Adirondack Mountains are in New York State.
  b. President Carter returned control of the Panama Canal to Panama.
  c. She missed the bus and arrives late.
  d. no mistakes

40. a. The childrens books are over there.
  b. There is not enough paper in the printer for the entire document.
  c. What's the weather forecast for today?
  d. no mistakes

For questions 41–45, choose the sentence that does NOT use the correct form of the commonly confused word. If there are no mistakes, select choice d.

41. a. If it's nice weather tomorrow, I plan to go for a hike.
  b. Some analysts think the stock market has seen it's best days.
  c. It's usually a good idea to purchase life insurance.
  d. no mistakes

42. a. She spoke too quickly to the group in the lobby.
  b. Can you attend this morning's meeting too?
  c. Save all of your files in to or three folders.
  d. no mistakes

43. a. When will you bring you're pictures to work?
  b. It is your responsibility to arrange the details.
  c. If you're planning to attend, please let me know in advance.
  d. no mistakes

44. a. Only their supervisor can answer those questions.
  b. There is a phone call for you.
  c. They're only two ways to handle that situation.
  d. no mistakes

45. a. They are the ones who deserve all the credit.
  b. This is the house that I told you about.
  c. Marie sent a gift to her grandmother, who is in the hospital.
  d. no mistakes

For questions 46–50, choose the sentence that is correct in both grammar and punctuation.

46. a. The trip was scheduled for Friday the family was excited.
  b. The trip was scheduled for Friday, and the family was excited.
  c. The trip was scheduled for. Friday the family was excited.
  d. The trip, was scheduled for Friday, and the family was excited.

47. **a.** They finished their lunch. Left the building. And returned at 1:30.

   b. They finished their lunch, left the building, and returns at 1:30.

   c. They finished their lunch, left the building, and returned at 1:30.

   d. They finished their lunch, left the building, and returning at 1:30.

48. **a.** Searching for her keys, Kira, knew she would be late.

   b. Searching for her keys Kira knew she would be late.

   c. Searching, for her keys and Kira knew she would be late.

   d. Searching for her keys, Kira knew she would be late.

49. **a.** The long-time residents in the community were proud of there school district.

   b. The long-time residents in the community were proud of their school district.

   c. The long-time residents in the community was proud of their school district.

   d. The long-time residents in the community, were proud of their school district.

50. **a.** Lisa, Dara, and Amy wanted to work together on the committee.

   b. Lisa Dara and Amy wants to work together on the committee.

   c. Lisa, Dara, and Amy wanting to work together on the committee.

   d. Lisa, Dara, and Amy have wants to work together on the committee.

ANSWERS

1. c. This is a sentence fragment.

2. c. This is a run-on sentence.

3. b. This is a sentence fragment.

4. d. There are no mistakes.

5. c. This is a run-on sentence.

6. c. This is a sentence fragment.

7. d. There are no mistakes.

8. b. This is a sentence fragment.

9. b. The commas set off the appositive in the sentence.

10. a. The comma sets off an introductory clause.

11. a. The comma sets off an introductory phrase.

12. c. The comma sets off the appositive in the sentence.

13. b. The commas separate items in a series.

14. a. *Spring* is not a proper noun, so it should not be capitalized.

15. c. The word *boys'* should not show possession; no apostrophe is needed.

16. a. A comma is needed to set off the introductory word, *occasionally*.

17. b. An apostrophe is needed before the last *s* in the word *elses* to show possession.

18. a. There should be periods after the abbreviation *U.S.*

19. b. The comma should be placed after the word *yours*.

20. d. This sentence is in the present tense.

21. c. The infinitive form of the verb is used in this sentence.

22. b. This sentence is in the past tense.

23. c. This sentence needs a verb that is in the past tense.

24. b. *Were* is in agreement with the plural subject *people*.

25. d. This sentence is in the future tense.

26. b. The correct form of the pronoun is me (objective case).

27. c. The correct pronoun is *who* because it refers to a person.

28. b. The pronoun *their* agrees with the plural subject, *George and Michael*.

29. a. The pronoun *them* agrees with the plural noun *flowers*.

30. d. *She and I* is the subject of the sentence, so the subjective case is needed.

31. d. There are no errors.

32. c. The word *that* should be *who* because it refers to people.

33. a. There should be a comma before the conjunction *and* in this sentence to separate two complete thoughts.

34. a. The contraction *doesn't* has an apostrophe.

35. c. The correct possessive pronoun is *theirs*, not *there's*.

36. d. There are no errors.

37. a. The correct verb form is *has broken*.

38. b. The correct verb form is *rang.*

39. c. Both verbs, *missed* and *arrives* should be in the past tense.

40. a. An apostrophe should be added before the *s* in *children's* to make it possessive.

41. b. This sentence uses the possessive form (with no apostrophe), *its.*

42. c. The form of this word is the number *two.*

43. a. This sentence should use the possessive form of the word *your.*

44. c. This sentence should use the adverb *there.*

45. d. There are no errors.

46. b. This choice uses the comma and the conjunction correctly. Choice **a** is a run-on sentence. Choice **c** contains sentence fragments. Choice **d** misuses commas.

47. c. The word *returned* is in the past tense, as are *finished* and *left.* Choice **a** contains sentence fragments. Choices **b** and **d** misuse verb tense.

48. d. The comma in this sentence correctly separates the introductory phrase. Choices **a** and **c** misuse commas. Choice **b** lacks punctuation.

49. b. This sentence uses the correct form of *their*, the correct verb, and the correct punctuation. The word *there* is used incorrectly in choice **a**. Choice **c** uses verb tense incorrectly. Choice **d** is an example of comma misuse.

50. a. This sentence uses the correct punctuation in a series and the correct verb form. Choices **b, c**, and **d** misuse commas and verb tense.

Spelling

Since accurate spelling is such an essential and important communication skill, it is always tested on Civil Service exams. In this chapter, you will find spelling rules, test tips, and practice exercises that will make the spelling section of the exam easier for you.

There is no "quick fix" for spelling. The secret to correct spelling is memorization. If you take the time to commit the words you encounter every day to memory, you will not only excel on this section of the test, but your correspondence and written work will be more clear and effective and look more professional.

Spelling tests are usually given in multiple-choice format. Typically, you will be given several possible spellings for a word and asked to identify the one that is correctly spelled. This can be a difficult task, even for the best speller, because you must be able to see very subtle differences between word spellings. The best way to prepare for a spelling test is to put your memorization skills into high gear, have a good grasp of spelling rules, and know the exceptions to those rules. The fundamental rules and their exceptions are outlined here.

SPELLING RULES AND EXCEPTIONS

The Rule	The Exception
Use *i* before *e*—as in *piece*.	Use *i* before *e* except after *c*—as in *receive* or *conceive*—or when *ei* sounds like *a*—as in *neighbor* or *weigh*.
When adding prefixes, do not change the spelling of the word—as in *unnecessary or misspell*	none
When adding suffixes, do not change the spelling of the word—as in *finally or usually*.	When a word ends in *y*, change the *y* to *i* before adding *ness* or *ly*—as in *readily* or *heaviness*. One-syllable words ending in *y* generally remain the same—as in *dryness* or *shyly*.
Drop the final e before adding a suffix that begins with a vowel—as in *caring* or *usable*.	Keep the final e to retain the soft sound of *c* or *g* preceding the *e*—as in *noticeable* or *courageous*.
Keep the final e before a suffix beginning with a consonant—as in *careful* or *careless*.	Words like *truly, argument, judgment,* or *acknowledgment* are exceptions.
When words end in *y* and a consonant precedes the *y*, change the *y* to *i* before adding a suffix with *i*—as in *hurried* or *funnier*.	none
When a suffix begins with a vowel, double the final consonant before the suffix if the word has only one syllable—as in *planning* or if the word ends with a single consonant preceded by a single vowel—as in *forgetting*.	If the accent is not on the last syllable, do not add a double consonant—as in *canceled* or *preferable*.

When spelling the plural form of a noun,

- add an *s*—as in *books* or *letters*.
- add an *es*—as in *boxes* or *lunches*. Nouns are normally made plural by adding an *s*. An *es* is added when there is an extra sound heard in words that end in *s, sh, ch, or x*—as in *dresses, birches, bushes,* or *boxes*.

- If the noun ends in a *y*, change the *y* to an *i* and add *es*—as in *salaries* or *ladies*.
- If the noun ends in *y* and is preceded by a vowel, just add *s*—as in *attorneys* or *monkeys*.

- If a noun ends in *f* or *fe*, add an *s*—as in *chiefs* or *roofs*.
- Some nouns that end in *f* or *fe* are formed by changing the *f* to *v* and adding *s* or *es*—as in *knives* or *leaves*.

- If a noun ends in *o* and is preceded by a vowel, add an *s*—as in *pianos* or *radios*.
- Some nouns that end in *o* preceded by a consonant are formed by adding *es*—as in *potatoes* or *tomatoes*.

- Plural or compound nouns can be spelled with an *s* or an *es*—as in *bookmarks* or *mailboxes*.
- When a noun and a modifier make a compound noun, the noun is made plural—as in *sisters-in-law* or *passers-by*.
- Numbers, letters, signs, and words that take the shape of words are spelled with an apostrophe and an *s*—*She received all A's on her report card. There are two o's and two m's in roommate.*

- Some plural nouns are irregular nouns and have to be memorized—as *children, men,* or *women*.
- A few compound nouns are irregular—as *six year olds* or *drive-ins*.
- Some nouns take the same form in the singular and the plural—as *deer, species,* or *sheep*.
- Some foreign words are formed as they were in their original languages—as *alumni* or *data*.
- Some foreign words may be spelled as they were in their original languages or by adding *s* or *es*—as *appendices/appendixes* or *indexes/indices*.
- Some foreign words are formed according to the ending of the word:
  * singular ending in *-is,* plural ending in *-es* —as in *analysis/analyses crisis/crises*
  * singular ending in *-um,* plural ending in *-a* —as in *curriculum/curricula*
  * singular ending in *-on,* plural ending in *-a* —as in *criterion/criteria*
  * singular ending in *-eau,* plural ending in *-eaux* —as in *beau/beaux*
  * singular ending in *-a,* plural ending in *-ae* —as in *formula/formulae*
  * singular ending in *-us,* plural ending in *-i* —as in *stimulus/stimuli*

When using *-cede, -ceed,* or *-sede,* memorize the following:

- There is only one English word ending in *-sede*: *supersede*.
- There are only three words ending in *-ceed*: *exceed, proceed,* and *succeed*.
- Other words that have the same sound end in *-cede*: *secede, precede,* and *concede*, for example.

HOW TO ANSWER SPELLING QUESTIONS

- Sound out the word in your mind. Remember that long vowels inside words usually are followed by single consonants—as in *sofa, total,* or *crime.* Short vowels inside words usually are followed by double consonants—as in *dribble, scissors,* or *toddler.*
- Give yourself auditory (listening) clues when you learn words. Say *Wed-nes-day* or *lis-ten* or *bus-i-ness* to yourself so that you remember to add the silent letters when you write the word.
- Look at each part of the word. See if there is a root, prefix, or suffix that will always be spelled the same way. For example, in the word *uninhabitable, un, in,* and *able* are always spelled the same. *Habit* is a self-contained root word that is easy to spell.
- Memorize as many spelling rules as you can, and know the exceptions to each rule.

Practice

Choose the word that is spelled correctly in the following sentences.

1. We went to an _____ of early Egyptian art.
   a. exibition
   b. exhibition
   c. excibition
   d. exebition

2. We will _____ go to the movies tonight.
   a. probly
   b. probbaly
   c. probely
   d. probably

3. We took _____ of pictures on our vacation.
   a. allot
   b. alot
   c. a lot
   d. alott

4. _____ answers on your test mean a better score for you.
   a. Accurate
   b. Acurate
   c. Accuret
   d. Accurit

5. The meteorologist predicted an _____ amount of wind today.

   a. exessive

   b. excesive

   c. excessive

   d. excesive

Answers

   1. b.

   2. d.

   3. c. *A lot*, meaning a great deal, is *always* two words. It should not be confused with *allot*, which means to assign, portion, or ration out.

   4. a.

   5. c.

► USING SPELLING LISTS

When you apply to take your Civil Service test, you may be given a list of spelling words to study. If so, here are some suggestions to make your studying a little easier and quicker.

   ► Cross out or discard any words that you already know for certain. Do not let them get in the way of the words you need to study.

   ► Divide the list into groups to study. The groups can be bunched as three, five, or seven words. Consider making flash cards for the words that you find the most difficult.

   ► Say the words as you read them. Spell them out in your mind so you can "hear" the spelling.

   ► Highlight or circle the tricky elements in each word.

   ► Quiz yourself and then check your spelling.

If you do not receive a list of spelling words to study, the following list is a good one to use. These words are typical of the words that appear on spelling exams.

achievement	doubtful	ninety
allege	eligible	noticeable
anxiety	enough	occasionally
appreciate	enthusiasm	occurred
asthma	equipped	offense
arraignment	exception	official
autonomous	fascinate	pamphlet
auxiliary	fatigue	parallel

brief	forfeit	personnel
ballistics	gauge	physician
barricade	grieve	politics
beauty	guilt	possess
beige	guarantee	privilege
business	harass	psychology
bureau	hazard	recommend
calm	height	referral
cashier	incident	rehearsal
capacity	indict	salary
cancel	initial	schedule
circuit	innocent	seize
colonel	irreverent	separate
comparatively	jeopardy	specific
courteous	knowledge	statistics
criticism	leisure	surveillance
custody	license	suspicious
cyclical	lieutenant	tentative
debt	maintenance	thorough
definitely	mathematics	transferred
descent	mortgage	withhold

▶ HOMOPHONES

Words that sound alike but have different meanings are called homophones. The following lists some of the most common homophones for you to study. It is best to study the spellings and the definitions until you have each word memorized.

ad: a shortened form of advertisement
add: to combine to form a sum

affect: to influence
effect: outcome or result

allowed: permitted
aloud: using a speaking voice

bare: without covering
bear: a large furry animal; to tolerate

board: a group of people in charge; a piece of wood
bored: to be tired of something

brake: to slow or stop something
break: to split or crack

build: to construct
billed: presented a statement of costs

cite: to quote as an authority or example
sight: ability to see; a scene
site: place or setting of something

council: a group that advises
counsel: advice; to advise

dew: moisture
do: to make or carry out
due: owed

fair: consistent with the rules; having a pleasing appearance; moderately good
fare: transportation charge; food and drink; to get along

for: because of or directed to
fore: located at or toward the front
four: the number between three and five

grate: reduce to fragments; make a harsh, grinding sound; irritate or annoy
great: very large in size

hear: to listen to
here: a specific place

heard: the past tense of *hear*
herd: a large group of animals

hole: an opening
whole: entire or complete

hour: sixty minutes
our: a pronoun showing possession

knew: past tense of *know*
new: recent

know: to understand
no: not permitted

lead: first or foremost position; a margin; information pointing toward a clue; to bring or guide
led: past tense of *lead*

leased: rented for a specific time period
least: lowest in importance or rank

lessen: made fewer in amount or quantity
lesson: exercise in which something is learned

made: past tense of *make*
maid: a female servant

meat: the edible part of an animal
meet: come together

passed: approved
past: previous, beforehand

peace: free from war
piece: a part of something

plain: level area; undecorated; clearly seen
plane: flat and even; a tool used to smooth wood; a shortened form of *airplane*

rain: water falling in drops
reign: period during which a monarch rules

right: correct or proper
rite: a ritual or ceremony
write: to record in print

role: function or position; character or part played by a performer
roll: to move forward by turning over

scene: the place something happens
seen: part of the verb *see*

soar: to fly or rise high into the air
sore: painful

stair: part of a flight of steps
stare: to look directly and fixedly

sweet: having a sugary taste
suite: series of connected rooms

their: ownership of something
there: a place
they're: a contraction of they are

threw: the past tense of throw; an act of motion
through: by means of, among or between

tide: variation of the level of bodies of water caused by gravitational forces
tied: fastened or secured

to: indicates direction
too: also
two: the number after one

vary: to change
very: complete; extremely

ware: articles of the same general kind, e.g., hardware, software
wear: to have or carry on the body
where: location or place

weather: condition of the atmosphere
whether: a possibility

wood: material that trees are made of
would: part of the verb *will*

Practice

Choose the word that is spelled correctly.

1. He stepped on the (break/brake) just before the stop sign.

2. The manager decided to (higher/hire) a few more employees.

3. Financial (council/counsel) is available for anyone who wants to invest money.

4. The speaker wanted to have all his (facts/fax) correct before he spoke to the audience.

5. No one (new/knew) exactly what had happened.

6. She considered it a (lessen/lesson) learned.

Answers

1. **brake.** A *brake* is a device used for stopping. *Break* means to damage or destroy something.

2. **hire.** To *hire* means to engage and pay someone for services rendered. *Higher* means to be in an elevated position, rank, or status.

3. **counsel.** *Counsel* is advice. A *council* is a group of people who meet for a purpose.

4. **facts.** *Facts* are knowledge or information based on truth. *Fax*—short for *facsimile*—is a document sent or received from a fax machine.

5. **knew.** *Knew* means having known something. *New* is the opposite of old.

6. **lesson.** A *lesson* is an experience or example from which knowledge or wisdom is gained. To *lessen* means to make less.

PRACTICE QUESTIONS

In each of the following questions, choose the correctly spelled word.

1.	ⓐ	ⓑ	ⓒ	ⓓ	26.	ⓐ	ⓑ	ⓒ	ⓓ
2.	ⓐ	ⓑ	ⓒ	ⓓ	27.	ⓐ	ⓑ	ⓒ	ⓓ
3.	ⓐ	ⓑ	ⓒ	ⓓ	28.	ⓐ	ⓑ	ⓒ	ⓓ
4.	ⓐ	ⓑ	ⓒ	ⓓ	29.	ⓐ	ⓑ	ⓒ	ⓓ
5.	ⓐ	ⓑ	ⓒ	ⓓ	30.	ⓐ	ⓑ	ⓒ	ⓓ
6.	ⓐ	ⓑ	ⓒ	ⓓ	31.	ⓐ	ⓑ	ⓒ	ⓓ
7.	ⓐ	ⓑ	ⓒ	ⓓ	32.	ⓐ	ⓑ	ⓒ	ⓓ
8.	ⓐ	ⓑ	ⓒ	ⓓ	33.	ⓐ	ⓑ	ⓒ	ⓓ
9.	ⓐ	ⓑ	ⓒ	ⓓ	34.	ⓐ	ⓑ	ⓒ	ⓓ
10.	ⓐ	ⓑ	ⓒ	ⓓ	35.	ⓐ	ⓑ	ⓒ	ⓓ
11.	ⓐ	ⓑ	ⓒ	ⓓ	36.	ⓐ	ⓑ	ⓒ	ⓓ
12.	ⓐ	ⓑ	ⓒ	ⓓ	37.	ⓐ	ⓑ	ⓒ	ⓓ
13.	ⓐ	ⓑ	ⓒ	ⓓ	38.	ⓐ	ⓑ	ⓒ	ⓓ
14.	ⓐ	ⓑ	ⓒ	ⓓ	39.	ⓐ	ⓑ	ⓒ	ⓓ
15.	ⓐ	ⓑ	ⓒ	ⓓ	40.	ⓐ	ⓑ	ⓒ	ⓓ
16.	ⓐ	ⓑ	ⓒ	ⓓ	41.	ⓐ	ⓑ	ⓒ	ⓓ
17.	ⓐ	ⓑ	ⓒ	ⓓ	42.	ⓐ	ⓑ	ⓒ	ⓓ
18.	ⓐ	ⓑ	ⓒ	ⓓ	43.	ⓐ	ⓑ	ⓒ	ⓓ
19.	ⓐ	ⓑ	ⓒ	ⓓ	44.	ⓐ	ⓑ	ⓒ	ⓓ
20.	ⓐ	ⓑ	ⓒ	ⓓ	45.	ⓐ	ⓑ	ⓒ	ⓓ
21.	ⓐ	ⓑ	ⓒ	ⓓ	46.	ⓐ	ⓑ	ⓒ	ⓓ
22.	ⓐ	ⓑ	ⓒ	ⓓ	47.	ⓐ	ⓑ	ⓒ	ⓓ
23.	ⓐ	ⓑ	ⓒ	ⓓ	48.	ⓐ	ⓑ	ⓒ	ⓓ
24.	ⓐ	ⓑ	ⓒ	ⓓ	49.	ⓐ	ⓑ	ⓒ	ⓓ
25.	ⓐ	ⓑ	ⓒ	ⓓ	50.	ⓐ	ⓑ	ⓒ	ⓓ

1. It is my _____ that municipal employees handle their jobs with great professionalism.
    a. beleif
    b. bilief
    c. belief
    d. beleaf

2. The accounting firm was _____ for fraudulent practices.
    a. prosecuted
    b. prossecuted
    c. prosecutted
    d. prosecuited

3. Every _____ has to be handled differently.
    a. sittuation
    b. situation
    c. situachun
    d. sitiation

4. It was a _____ day for the department's annual picnic.
    a. superb
    b. supperb
    c. supurb
    d. sepurb

5. To be elected _____, candidates must have a solid background in law enforcement.
    a. sherrif
    b. sherriff
    c. sherif
    d. sheriff

6. To be hired for the job, he needed to have _____ ability.
    a. mechinical
    b. mechanical
    c. mechenical
    d. machanical

7. The agents were searching for _____ cargo on the airplane.
    a. elicitt
    b. ellicit
    c. illicet
    d. illicit

8. There will be an immediate _____ into the cause of the accident.

   a. inquiry

   b. inquirry

   c. enquirry

   d. enquery

9. The union workers' contract could not be _____ before the calendar year ended.

   a. terminated

   b. termenated

   c. terrminated

   d. termanated

10. A _____ can be obtained at the town hall.

   a. lisense

   b. lisence

   c. lycence

   d. license

11. In many states, passing a road test requires drivers to _____ park.

   a. paralel

   b. paralell

   c. parallal

   d. parallel

12. The paramedics attempted to _____ the victim.

   a. stabilize

   b. stablize

   c. stableize

   d. stableise

13. The attorney asked a question that was _____ to the case; the judge overruled it.

   a. irelevent

   b. irelevant

   c. irrelevant

   d. irrelevent

14. The mayor highlighted the _____ statistics during her campaign speech.

   a. encouredging

   b. encouraging

   c. incurraging

   d. incouraging

For each of the following questions, choose the misspelled word. If there are no mistakes, select choice d.

15. a. radios
    b. leaves
    c. alumni
    d. no mistakes

16. a. anouncement
    b. advisement
    c. description
    d. no mistakes

17. a. omission
    b. aisle
    c. litrature
    d. no mistakes

18. a. informal
    b. servent
    c. comfortable
    d. no mistakes

19. a. vegetable
    b. width
    c. variation
    d. no mistakes

20. a. twentieth
    b. fortieth
    c. ninetieth
    d. no mistakes

21. a. association
    b. unecessary
    c. illegal
    d. no mistakes

22. a. villin
    b. volunteer
    c. voracious
    d. no mistakes

23. a. hindrence
   b. equipped
   c. possessive
   d. no mistakes

24. a. procedure
   b. judgment
   c. testamony
   d. no mistakes

25. a. explicit
   b. abduct
   c. rotate
   d. no mistakes

26. a. through
   b. threw
   c. thorough
   d. no mistakes

27. a. quantaty
   b. quality
   c. quaint
   d. no mistakes

28. a. requirement
   b. reverence
   c. resistent
   d. no mistakes

29. a. incorporate
   b. contridict
   c. exhale
   d. no mistakes

30. a. pertain
   b. reversel
   c. memorization
   d. no mistakes

31. a. marshal
   b. martial
   c. tyrenny
   d. no mistakes

32. a. optimum
b. palpable
c. plunder
d. no mistakes

33. a. ravinous
b. miraculous
c. wondrous
d. no mistakes

34. a. phenomonal
b. emulate
c. misconception
d. no mistakes

35. a. mischief
b. temperture
c. lovable
d. no mistakes

36. a. stadium
b. competitor
c. atheletic
d. no mistakes

For the questions 37–50, choose the correct homophone.

37. My favorite _____ is peach pie with vanilla ice cream.
a. desert
b. dessert

38. While nuclear energy is efficient, storing nuclear _____ is always a problem.
a. waste
b. waist

39. The price for the carpet was _____.
a. fair
b. fare

40. This is the _____ of the new art museum.
a. sight
b. cite
c. site

41. Come _____ the park later this evening to see the sunset.
   a. buy
   b. bye
   c. by

42. This is the _____ book George has read.
   a. fourth
   b. forth

43. The acoustics in the auditorium made it easy for the audience to _____ the melodic sounds of the soloist.
   a. here
   b. hear

44. Our choice to stay in the comfortable, cozy _____ house was a good decision.
   a. guessed
   b. guest

45. Have dinner with us at the restaurant; we'll meet you _____.
   a. they're
   b. their
   c. there

46. May I have a _____ of cheese?
   a. piece
   b. peace

47. All children have the _____ to an education.
   a. write
   b. rite
   c. right

48. It is a good idea to exercise on a _____ bicycle during inclement weather.
   a. stationery
   b. stationary

49. At the beach, we went digging for clams and _____.
   a. mussels
   b. muscles

50. We _____ the exit and had to turn around.
   a. past
   b. passed

ANSWERS

1. **c.** belief
2. **a.** prosecuted
3. **b.** situation
4. **a.** superb
5. **d.** sheriff
6. **b.** mechanical
7. **d.** illicit. This word should not be confused with *elicit*, which means to draw out or extract.
8. **a.** inquiry
9. **a.** terminated
10. **d.** license
11. **d.** parallel
12. **a.** stabilize
13. **c.** irrelevant
14. **b.** encouraging
15. **d.** no mistakes
16. **a.** announcement
17. **c.** literature
18. **b.** servant
19. **d.** no mistakes
20. **d.** no mistakes
21. **b.** unnecessary
22. **a.** villain
23. **a.** hindrance
24. **c.** testimony
25. **d.** no mistakes
26. **d.** no mistakes
27. **a.** quantity
28. **c.** resistant
29. **b.** contradict
30. **b.** reversal
31. **c.** tyranny
32. **d.** no mistakes
33. **a.** ravenous
34. **a.** phenomenal
35. **b.** temperature
36. **c.** athletic
37. **b.** *Dessert* is an after-dinner treat; a *desert* is an arid land.
38. **a.** *Waste* means material that is rejected during a process; the *waist* is the middle of the body.

39. **a.** *Fair* means equitable; a *fare* is a transportation fee.

40. **c.** *Site* refers to a place; *cite* means to refer to; *sight* is the ability to see.

41. **c.** *By* means near; *bye* is used to express farewell; *buy* means to purchase.

42. **a.** *Fourth* refers to the number four; *forth* means forward.

43. **b.** *Hear* means to perceive sound with the ear; *here* is a location, place, or position.

44. **b.** A *guest* is one who is a recipient of hospitality. *Guessed* is to predict without significant information.

45. **c.** *There* refers to a place; *their* is a possessive pronoun; *they're* is a contraction for they are.

46. **a.** A *piece* is a portion; *peace* means calm or quiet.

47. **c.** A *right* is a privilege; to *write* is to put words on paper; a *rite* is a ceremonial ritual.

48. **b.** *Stationary* means standing still; *stationery* is writing paper.

49. **a.** *Mussels* are marine animals; *muscles* are body tissues.

50. **b.** *Passed* is the past tense of pass; *past* means a time gone by.

Practice Test 1

Now that you have studied all of the chapters in this book, you should be able to use what you have learned to answer the questions on these sample examinations. This chapter contains your first practice test. Take Practice Test 1. Be sure to review the questions you answered incorrectly by going back and studying the corresponding material from earlier chapters. Then try it again. Next, take Practice Test 2 in the last chapter of this book. Each test should take about 30–45 minutes to complete. Good luck!

Use the answer grid on the following page to fill in your answers to the questions.

1.	ⓐ ⓑ ⓒ ⓓ	26.	ⓐ ⓑ ⓒ ⓓ
2.	ⓐ ⓑ ⓒ ⓓ	27.	ⓐ ⓑ ⓒ ⓓ
3.	ⓐ ⓑ ⓒ ⓓ	28.	ⓐ ⓑ ⓒ ⓓ
4.	ⓐ ⓑ ⓒ ⓓ	29.	ⓐ ⓑ ⓒ ⓓ
5.	ⓐ ⓑ ⓒ ⓓ	30.	ⓐ ⓑ ⓒ ⓓ
6.	ⓐ ⓑ ⓒ ⓓ	31.	ⓐ ⓑ ⓒ ⓓ
7.	ⓐ ⓑ ⓒ ⓓ	32.	ⓐ ⓑ ⓒ ⓓ
8.	ⓐ ⓑ ⓒ ⓓ	33.	ⓐ ⓑ ⓒ ⓓ
9.	ⓐ ⓑ ⓒ ⓓ	34.	ⓐ ⓑ ⓒ ⓓ
10.	ⓐ ⓑ ⓒ ⓓ	35.	ⓐ ⓑ ⓒ ⓓ
11.	ⓐ ⓑ ⓒ ⓓ	36.	ⓐ ⓑ ⓒ ⓓ
12.	ⓐ ⓑ ⓒ ⓓ	37.	ⓐ ⓑ ⓒ ⓓ
13.	ⓐ ⓑ ⓒ ⓓ	38.	ⓐ ⓑ ⓒ ⓓ
14.	ⓐ ⓑ ⓒ ⓓ	39.	ⓐ ⓑ ⓒ ⓓ
15.	ⓐ ⓑ ⓒ ⓓ	40.	ⓐ ⓑ ⓒ ⓓ
16.	ⓐ ⓑ ⓒ ⓓ	41.	ⓐ ⓑ ⓒ ⓓ
17.	ⓐ ⓑ ⓒ ⓓ	42.	ⓐ ⓑ ⓒ ⓓ
18.	ⓐ ⓑ ⓒ ⓓ	43.	ⓐ ⓑ ⓒ ⓓ
19.	ⓐ ⓑ ⓒ ⓓ	44.	ⓐ ⓑ ⓒ ⓓ
20.	ⓐ ⓑ ⓒ ⓓ	45.	ⓐ ⓑ ⓒ ⓓ
21.	ⓐ ⓑ ⓒ ⓓ	46.	ⓐ ⓑ ⓒ ⓓ
22.	ⓐ ⓑ ⓒ ⓓ	47.	ⓐ ⓑ ⓒ ⓓ
23.	ⓐ ⓑ ⓒ ⓓ	48.	ⓐ ⓑ ⓒ ⓓ
24.	ⓐ ⓑ ⓒ ⓓ	49.	ⓐ ⓑ ⓒ ⓓ
25.	ⓐ ⓑ ⓒ ⓓ	50.	ⓐ ⓑ ⓒ ⓓ

Choose the correct vocabulary word to complete each of the following sentences.

  1. The newspaper _____ the statement made in the article because it was incorrectly stated.
   a. abolished
   b. invalidated
   c. retracted
   d. annulled

  2. The proposition was read, and the committee was asked to vote on the issue; Connor decided to _____ from the vote.
   a. tackle
   b. undermine
   c. abstain
   d. destabilize

  3. Typically, computer designs reach _____ within six months.
   a. division
   b. discord
   c. obsolescence
   d. secrecy

  4. For information about making a sound investment, you should get advice from a/an _____.
   a. prospectus
   b. entrepreneur
   c. teller
   d. cashier

  5. The new congressman was considered a _____ because he refused to follow his party's platform on nearly every issue.
   a. mentor
   b. maverick
   c. protagonist
   d. visionary

  6. School calendars were originally based on a/an _____ lifestyle, where all family members needed to be available to help in the fields.
   a. business
   b. technological
   c. scientific
   d. agrarian

7. The project seemed both _____ and beneficial, and the office staff supported it enthusiastically.
   a. implacable
   b. feasible
   c. savory
   d. irreparable

8. Ethan, a _____ young worker, diligently replaced all of the research files at the end of every day.
   a. erudite
   b. insightful
   c. meticulous
   d. sagacious

9. His _____ behavior made him seem childish and immature.
   a. beguiling
   b. receding
   c. forlorn
   d. puerile

10. The _____ young woman gave generously to many worthy causes.
   a. incisive
   b. benevolent
   c. gregarious
   d. personable

11. _____, the pediatric nurse fed the premature baby.
   a. Carelessly
   b. Precariously
   c. Gingerly
   d. Wantonly

12. The furniture in the attic turned out to be a veritable _____ of valuable antiques.
   a. reproof
   b. bonanza
   c. censure
   d. rubble

13. Choosing to _____ her estate to the literacy foundation, she was able to help those who could not read.
   a. confiscate
   b. eliminate
   c. bequeath
   d. extract

14. Her haughty and _____manner was not appealing to her constituents.

   a. poignant

   b. nocturnal

   c. amicable

   d. supercilious

15. _____donations from a generous but anonymous benefactor were received every year at the children's hospital.

   a. Magnanimous

   b. Parsimonious

   c. Prudent

   d. Diplomatic

Read the following passage and respond to the questions that follow.

Today, bicycles are elegantly simple machines that are common all over the globe. Many people ride bicycles for recreation while others use them as a means of transportation. The first bicycle, called a *draisienne*, was invented in Germany in 1818 by Baron Karl de Draid de Sauerbrun. Because it was made of wood, the *draisienne* was not very durable nor did it have pedals. Riders moved it by pushing their feet against the ground.

In 1839, Kirkpatrick Macmillan, a Scottish blacksmith, invented a much better bicycle. Macmillan's machine had tires with iron rims to keep them from getting worn down. He also used foot-operated cranks similar to pedals so his bicycle could be ridden at a quick pace. It did not look much like the modern bicycle because its back wheel was substantially larger than its front wheel. Although Macmillan's bicycle could be ridden easily, they were never produced in large numbers.

In 1861, Frenchman Pierre Michaux and his brother Ernest invented a bicycle with an improved crank mechanism. They called their bicycle, a velocipede, but most people called it a bone shaker because of the jarring effect of the wood and iron frame. Despite the unflattering nickname, the velocipede was a hit and the Michaux family made hundreds of the machines annually. Most of them were for fun-seeking young people.

Ten years later, James Starley, an English inventor, made several innovations that revolutionized bicycle design. He made the front wheel many times larger than the back wheel, put a gear on the pedals to make the bicycle more efficient, and lightened the wheels by using wire spokes. Although this bicycle was much lighter and less tiring to ride, it was still clumsy, extremely top-heavy, and ridden mostly for entertainment.

It was not until 1874 that the first truly modern bicycle appeared on the scene. Invented by another Englishman, H. J. Lawson, this safety bicycle would look familiar to today's cyclists. The safety bicycle had equalized wheels, which made it much less prone to toppling over. Lawson also attached a chain to the pedals to drive the rear wheel. By 1893, the safety bicycle had been further improved with air-filled rubber tires, a diamond-shaped frame, and easy braking. With the improvements provided by Lawson, bicycles became extremely popular and useful for transportation. Today they are built, used, and enjoyed all over the world.

16. There is enough information in this passage to show that
   a. several people contributed to the development of the modern bicycle.
   b. only a few velocipedes built by the Michaus family are still in existence.
   c. for most of the nineteenth century, few people rode bicycles just for fun.
   d. bicycles with wheels of different sizes cannot be ridden easily.

17. The first person to use a gear system on bicycles was
   a. H. J. Lawson.
   b. Kirkpatrick Macmillan.
   c. Pierre Michaux.
   d. James Starley.

18. This passage was most likely written in order to
   a. persuade readers to use bicycles for transportation.
   b. describe the problems that bicycle manufacturers encounter.
   c. compare bicycles used for fun with bicycles used for transportation.
   d. tell readers a little about the history of the bicycle.

19. Macmillan added iron rims to the tires of his bicycle to
   a. add weight to the bicycle.
   b. make the tires last longer.
   c. make the ride less bumpy.
   d. made the ride less tiring.

20. Read the following sentence from the fourth paragraph:

Ten years later, James Starley, an English inventor, made several innovations that *revolutionized* bicycle design.

As it is used in the sentence, the word *revolutionized* most nearly means
   a. canceled.
   b. transformed.
   c. maintained.
   d. preserved.

21. Which of the following statements from the passage represents the writer's *opinion*?
   a. The safety bicycle would look familiar to today's cyclists.
   b. Two hundred years ago, bicycles did not even exist.
   c. The Michaux brothers called their bicycle a velocipede.
   d. Macmillan's machine had tires with iron rims.

Read the directions for each of the following questions carefully and select the word that is the synonym or antonym for the word provided.

22. A synonym for *apathetic* is
- **a.** pitiable.
- **b.** indifferent.
- **c.** suspicious.
- **d.** evasive.

23. A synonym for *surreptitious* is
- **a.** expressive.
- **b.** secretive.
- **c.** emotional.
- **d.** artistic.

24. An antonym for *deterrent* is
- **a.** encouragement.
- **b.** obstacle.
- **c.** proponent.
- **d.** discomfort.

25. An antonym for *impertinent* is
- **a.** reverential.
- **b.** rude.
- **c.** relentless.
- **d.** polite.

26. A synonym for *animated* is
- **a.** abbreviated.
- **b.** civil.
- **c.** secret.
- **d.** lively.

27. A synonym for *augment* is
- **a.** repeal.
- **b.** evaluate.
- **c.** increase.
- **d.** criticize.

28. An antonym for *ludicrous* is
- **a.** absurd.
- **b.** somber.
- **c.** reasonable.
- **d.** charitable.

29. An antonym for *archaic* is
   a. tangible.
   b. modern.
   c. ancient.
   d. haunted.

30. A synonym for *vindictive* is
   a. outrageous.
   b. insulting.
   c. spiteful.
   d. offensive.

Answer each of the following grammar and usage questions.

31. Which of the following sentences uses the correct pronoun form?
   a. Do you think you will work with Jason or I on this project?
   b. Do you think you will work with Jason or me on this project?
   c. Do you think you will work with Jason or she on this project?
   d. Do you think you will work with Jason or he on this project?

32. Which of the following sentences is correctly punctuated?
   a. Charlotte, who ran in the Boston Marathon last year will compete in this years New York Marathon.
   b. Charlotte who ran in the Boston Marathon, last year, will compete in this year's New York Marathon.
   c. Charlotte who ran in the Boston Marathon last year, will compete in this years New York Marathon.
   d. Charlotte, who ran in the Boston Marathon last year, will compete in this year's New York Marathon.

33. Which of the following sentences is capitalized correctly?
   a. The Governor gave a speech at the fourth of July picnic, which was held at morgan's beach.
   b. The Governor gave a speech at the Fourth of July picnic, which was held at Morgan's beach.
   c. The governor gave a speech at the Fourth of July picnic, which was held at Morgan's Beach.
   d. The governor gave a speech at the fourth of july picnic, which was held at Morgan's Beach.

34. Which of the following sentences uses the correct verb form?
    a. Before learning to read, my sister takes me to the public library.
    b. Before learning to read, my sister will take me to the public library.
    c. Before learning to read, my sister took me to the public library.
    d. Before learning to read, my sister has took me to the pubic library.

35. Which of the following sentences shows subject/verb agreement?
    a. The art professor, along with several of her students, is planning to attend the gallery opening tomorrow evening.
    b. The art professor, along with several of her students, are planning to attend the gallery opening tomorrow evening.
    c. The art professor, along with several of her students, plan to attend the gallery opening tomorrow evening.
    d. The art professor, along with several of her students, have planned to attend the gallery opening tomorrow evening.

36. In which of the following sentences is the verb NOT in agreement with the subject?
    a. Where are the forms you want me to fill out?
    b. Which is the correct form?
    c. Here is the forms you need to complete.
    d. There are two people who still need to complete the form.

37. In which of the following sentences is the pronoun incorrect?
    a. Francine can run much faster than me.
    b. Erin and Bob are painting the house by themselves.
    c. Five members of the team and I will represent our school.
    d. Our neighbors gave us some tomatoes from their garden.

38. Which of the following sentences uses the correct verb form?
    a. Only one of the many problems were solved.
    b. Only one of the many problems was solved.
    c. Only one of the many problems been solved.
    d. Only one of the many problems are solved.

39. Which of the following sentences uses punctuation correctly?
    a. Dr. Richard K Brown, CEO of the company, will speak to the scientists at Brookhaven National Laboratory on Wed at 9:00 AM.
    b. Dr Richard K Brown, C.E.O. of the company, will speak to the scientists at the Brookhaven National Laboratory on Wed. at 9:00 A.M.
    c. Dr. Richard K. Brown, C.E.O. of the company, will speak to the scientists at the Brookhaven National Laboratory on Wed. at 9:00 A.M.
    d. Dr. Richard K. Brown, C.E.O. of the company, will speak to the scientists at the Brookhaven National Laboratory on Wed at 9:00 AM.

40. Which of the following sentences is NOT a run-on sentence?
    a. He was from a small town, he moved to a very large city.
    b. He was from a small town he moved to a very large city.
    c. He was from a small town, but he moved to a very large city.
    d. He was from a small town but he moved to a very large city.

Choose the correctly spelled word to complete each of the following sentences.

41. Each of the new employees has similar _____.
    a. asspirations
    b. asparations
    c. aspirrations
    d. aspirations

42. The president and the vice president were a _____ pair.
    a. compatible
    b. compatable
    c. commpatible
    d. compatibel

43. I was skeptical of the claims made by the _____ salesman.
    a. loquatious
    b. loquacious
    c. loquacius
    d. loquecious

44. Who is your immediate _____?
    a. supervisor
    b. supervizor
    c. superviser
    d. supervizer

45. There are two types of _____: viral and bacterial.
    a. neumonia
    b. pnumonia
    c. pnemonia
    d. pneumonia

Choose the misspelled word in the questions below. If there are no mistakes, select choice d.

46. a. illuminate
   b. enlighten
   c. clarify
   d. no mistakes

47. a. abolish
   b. forfit
   c. negate
   d. no mistakes

48. a. zoology
   b. meterology
   c. anthropology
   d. no mistakes

49. a. ajournment
   b. tournament
   c. confinement
   d. no mistakes

50. a. vague
   b. trepidation
   c. vengence
   d. no mistakes

ANSWERS

1. **c.** To *retract* something is to take it back or disavow it. This is the term usually applied to disavowing something erroneous or libelous printed in a newspaper.

2. **c.** To *abstain* means to refrain from something by one's own choice.

3. **c.** *Obsolescence* is the state of being outdated.

4. **a.** A *prospectus* is a published report of a business and its plans for a program or offering.

5. **b.** A *maverick* is a political independent, nonconformist, or free spirit.

6. **d.** *Agrarian* means having to do with agriculture or farming.

7. **b.** To be *feasible* is to be practical, manageable, convenient, or serviceable.

8. **c.** *Meticulous* means extremely and excessively concerned with details.

9. **d.** *Puerile* means to be of or like a child; to be boyish, trifling, or silly.

10. **b.** A *benevolent* person is one who is charitable, giving.

11. **c.** To handle a baby *gingerly* would be to handle it delicately and with great caution.

12. **b.** A *bonanza* is a source of great wealth or prosperity.

13. **c.** To *bequeath* something is to pass it to another when you die.

14. **d.** To be *supercilious* means to show arrogant superiority and disdain for those one views as unworthy.

15. **a.** *Magnanimous* donations are noble in mind or heart.

16. **a.** Each paragraph of the passage describes an inventor whose inventions became more and more advanced. There is no evidence to support choice **b.** Choices **c** and **d** are incorrect because they both make statements that, according to the passage, are untrue.

17. **d.** The fourth paragraph states that James Starley added a gear to the pedals.

18. **d.** The passage gives the history of the bicycle. Choice **a** is incorrect because few opinions are included in the passage. There is no support for choices **b** and **c**.

19. **b.** This information is clearly stated in the second paragraph. The iron rims kept the tires from wearing down, and the tires lasted longer. Choice **a** is incorrect because although the iron rims probably did make the machine heavier, that was not Macmillan's goal. Choice **c** is incorrect because no information is given about whether iron-rimmed or wooden tires moved more smoothly. There is no support for choice **d**.

20. **b.** Based on the paragraph, this is the only possible choice. Starley *revolutionized* the bicycle; he made many innovative changes, thereby transforming the form and shape of the bicycle. Based on the context, the other choices are incorrect.

21. **a.** This is the only choice that states an opinion. The writer cannot be certain that the safety bicycle would look familiar to today's cyclists; it is his or her opinion that this is so. The other choices are presented as facts.

22. **b.** To be *apathetic* is to show little emotion or interest; to be *indifferent* is to have no particular interest or concern.

23. **b.** *Surreptitious* is acting in a stealthy or *secretive* manner.

24. **a.** A *deterrent* prevents or discourages; *encouragement* inspires or heartens.

25. **d.** Someone who is *impertinent* is rude; someone who is *polite* is courteous.

26. **d.** To be *animated* is to be filled with activity or vigor; *lively* is to be filled with energy.

27. **c.** To *augment* means to *increase* or expand in size or extent.

28. **c.** To be *ludicrous* is to be absurd; to be *reasonable* is to be rational.

29. **b.** *Archaic* means ancient or outdated; *modern* is current or contemporary.

30. **c.** To be *vindictive* is to be vengeful; to be *spiteful* means to be malicious.

31. **b.** *Jason or me* is the object of the sentence; the objective pronoun *me* is used.

32. **d.** In this sentence, the appositive—*who ran in the Boston Marathon last year*—describes Charlotte and is separated from the rest of the sentence with commas. The word year's is possessive and has an apostrophe.

33. **c.** All proper nouns—*Fourth of July* and *Morgan's Beach*—are capitalized correctly in this sentence.

34. **c.** This sentence is in the past tense and uses the verb *took*.

35. **a.** The subject of the sentence *art professor* is singular and takes the singular verb *is planning*.

36. **c.** The subject *forms* should take the plural verb *are*, not the singular is.

37. **a.** If completed, the sentence would read, Francine can run much faster than *I* can run, therefore the subjective pronoun *I* is used.

38. **b.** The subject of the sentence *one* takes the singular verb *was solved*.

39. **c.** Periods are correctly placed after all abbreviations in this sentence.

40. **c.** This sentence has a comma before the conjunction *but* which correctly connects the two complete thoughts in the sentence.

41. **d.** The correct spelling is *aspirations*.

42. **a.** The correct spelling is *compatible*.

43. **b.** The correct spelling is *loquacious*.

44. **a.** The correct spelling is *supervisor*.

45. **d.** The correct spelling is *pneumonia*.

46. **d.** no mistakes

47. **b.** The correct spelling is *forfeit*.

48. **b.** The correct spelling is *meteorology*.

49. **a.** The correct spelling is *adjournment*.

50. **c.** The correct spelling is *vengeance*.

Practice Test 2

This second practice test will give you another chance to measure your skills. By the time you have finished all of the chapters in this book and completed the two practice tests, you should see real progress in your vocabulary, reading comprehension, and spelling skills. This test should take about 30–45 minutes to complete.

Use the answer grid on the following page to fill in your answers to the questions.

1.	ⓐ	ⓑ	ⓒ	ⓓ	26.	ⓐ	ⓑ	ⓒ	ⓓ
2.	ⓐ	ⓑ	ⓒ	ⓓ	27.	ⓐ	ⓑ	ⓒ	ⓓ
3.	ⓐ	ⓑ	ⓒ	ⓓ	28.	ⓐ	ⓑ	ⓒ	ⓓ
4.	ⓐ	ⓑ	ⓒ	ⓓ	29.	ⓐ	ⓑ	ⓒ	ⓓ
5.	ⓐ	ⓑ	ⓒ	ⓓ	30.	ⓐ	ⓑ	ⓒ	ⓓ
6.	ⓐ	ⓑ	ⓒ	ⓓ	31.	ⓐ	ⓑ	ⓒ	ⓓ
7.	ⓐ	ⓑ	ⓒ	ⓓ	32.	ⓐ	ⓑ	ⓒ	ⓓ
8.	ⓐ	ⓑ	ⓒ	ⓓ	33.	ⓐ	ⓑ	ⓒ	ⓓ
9.	ⓐ	ⓑ	ⓒ	ⓓ	34.	ⓐ	ⓑ	ⓒ	ⓓ
10.	ⓐ	ⓑ	ⓒ	ⓓ	35.	ⓐ	ⓑ	ⓒ	ⓓ
11.	ⓐ	ⓑ	ⓒ	ⓓ	36.	ⓐ	ⓑ	ⓒ	ⓓ
12.	ⓐ	ⓑ	ⓒ	ⓓ	37.	ⓐ	ⓑ	ⓒ	ⓓ
13.	ⓐ	ⓑ	ⓒ	ⓓ	38.	ⓐ	ⓑ	ⓒ	ⓓ
14.	ⓐ	ⓑ	ⓒ	ⓓ	39.	ⓐ	ⓑ	ⓒ	ⓓ
15.	ⓐ	ⓑ	ⓒ	ⓓ	40.	ⓐ	ⓑ	ⓒ	ⓓ
16.	ⓐ	ⓑ	ⓒ	ⓓ	41.	ⓐ	ⓑ	ⓒ	ⓓ
17.	ⓐ	ⓑ	ⓒ	ⓓ	42.	ⓐ	ⓑ	ⓒ	ⓓ
18.	ⓐ	ⓑ	ⓒ	ⓓ	43.	ⓐ	ⓑ	ⓒ	ⓓ
19.	ⓐ	ⓑ	ⓒ	ⓓ	44.	ⓐ	ⓑ	ⓒ	ⓓ
20.	ⓐ	ⓑ	ⓒ	ⓓ	45.	ⓐ	ⓑ	ⓒ	ⓓ
21.	ⓐ	ⓑ	ⓒ	ⓓ	46.	ⓐ	ⓑ	ⓒ	ⓓ
22.	ⓐ	ⓑ	ⓒ	ⓓ	47.	ⓐ	ⓑ	ⓒ	ⓓ
23.	ⓐ	ⓑ	ⓒ	ⓓ	48.	ⓐ	ⓑ	ⓒ	ⓓ
24.	ⓐ	ⓑ	ⓒ	ⓓ	49.	ⓐ	ⓑ	ⓒ	ⓓ
25.	ⓐ	ⓑ	ⓒ	ⓓ	50.	ⓐ	ⓑ	ⓒ	ⓓ

Choose the correct vocabulary word for each of the following sentences.

1. Portland's oldest citizen was _____; he refused to leave his home, even when he was warned of rising floodwaters.
   a. recitative
   b. redundant
   c. repatriated
   d. recalcitrant

2. Michael and Brendan had such terrific _____ ; they always seemed to know, without being told, what the other felt.
   a. altercation
   b. equilibrium
   c. rapport
   d. symmetry

3. The politician's _____ voice detailed the many projects he planned to tackle once he was in office.
   a. clamorous
   b. flocculent
   c. affable
   d. fervent

4. The audience puzzled over the _____ remark made by the mayoral candidate.
   a. obvious
   b. cryptic
   c. shrewd
   d. conniving

5. She shed _____ tears when she heard the tragic news.
   a. copious
   b. scant
   c. nonchalant
   d. genteel

6. After graduation, Charles requested a/an _____ so that he did not have to pay his school loans immediately.
   a. surrogate
   b. deferment
   c. tincture
   d. improvement

7. The non-profit agency bought office supplies using a tax _____ number.
   a. liability
   b. exempt
   c. information
   d. accountability

8. With this group of _____ personalities, she was sure her party would be a success.
   a. scintillating
   b. mundane
   c. irradiated
   d. burnished

9. Her _____ remarks were not taken seriously by anyone on the nominating committee.
   a. porous
   b. obsessive
   c. frivolous
   d. durable

10. A key reference book detailing eyewitness accounts had to have _____ updates when new information surfaced.
   a. subsequent
   b. personable
   c. rote
   d. steadfast

11. The National Parks Service, in _____ with its mission, preserves the great outdoors for all to enjoy.
   a. contention
   b. amnesty
   c. conflict
   d. accordance

12. The exhibit at the botanical gardens is an unusual collection of cacti and other _____ from around the world.
   a. perennials
   b. succulents
   c. annuals
   d. tubers

13. Although the freeway system continues to grow, it often cannot keep pace with a _____ population.

   a. burgeoning

   b. beckoning

   c. capitulating

   d. exasperating

14. With admirable _____, the renowned orator spoke to the crowd gathered in the lecture hall.

   a. toil

   b. ado

   c. finesse

   d. tedium

15. The _____ advice offered by his friend saved him from making a grave mistake.

   a. insensitive

   b. judicious

   c. metaphorical

   d. unorthodox

Read the following passage and respond to the questions that follow.

Although many companies offer tuition reimbursement, most companies reimburse employees only for classes that are relevant to their position. This is a very limiting policy. A company that reimburses employees for all college credit courses—whether job-related or not—offers a service not only to the employees but to the entire company and greater community.

One good reason for giving employees unconditional tuition reimbursement is that it shows the company's dedication to its employees. In today's economy, where job security is a thing of the past and employees feel more and more expendable, it is important for a company to demonstrate to its employees that it cares. The best way to do this is with concrete investments in the employees and their futures.

In turn, this dedication to the betterment of company employees will create greater employee loyalty. A company that releases funds to pay for the education of its employees will get its money back by having employees stay with the company longer. Employee turnover will be reduced because even the employees who do not take advantage of the tuition reimbursement program will be more loyal to their company—just knowing that their company cares enough to pay for their education invokes loyalty.

Most importantly, the company that has an unrestricted tuition reimbursement program will have higher quality employees. Although these companies do indeed run the risk of losing money on employees who go on to another job in a different company as soon as they get their degree, more often than not, the employee will stay with the company. And even if employees do leave after graduation, it generally takes several years to complete any degree program. If the employee leaves upon graduation, the employer will have had a more sophisticated, more intelligent, and therefore more valuable and productive employee during that employee's tenure with the company. If the employee stays, that education will doubly benefit the company. Not only is the employee more educated, but now that employee can be promoted, and the company does not have to fill a high-level vacancy from the outside. Vacancies can be filled by people who already know the company well.

Though unconditional tuition reimbursement requires a significant investment on the employer's part, it is perhaps one of the wisest investments a company can make.

16. According to the passage, unconditional tuition reimbursement is good for which of the following reasons?
  a. Employees get a cheaper education.
  b. Employees become more valuable.
  c. Employees can find better jobs.
  d. Employers lose a great deal of money.

17. Which of the following statements, from the passage, is NOT an opinion?
  a. The best way to do this is with concrete investments in them.
  b. Most importantly, the company that has an unrestricted tuition reimbursement program will have higher quality employees.
  c. Although many companies offer tuition reimbursement, most companies reimburse employees only for classes that are relevant to their position.
  d. A company that puts out funds to pay for the education of its employees will get its money back by having employees stay with the company longer.

18. The author's reason for writing this passage was to
  a. entertain the reader.
  b. narrate a story.
  c. explain tuition reimbursement.
  d. persuade the reader.

19. The writer most likely uses the word *wisest* in the last sentence, rather than words such as *profitable*, *practical*, or *beneficial*, because
  a. wisdom is associated with education, the subject of the passage.
  b. the writer is trying to appeal to people who are already highly educated.
  c. education could not be considered practical.
  d. the word *beneficial* is too abstract for readers to comprehend.

20. Which of the following words best describes the tone of this passage?
  a. insincere
  b. deceitful
  c. optimistic
  d. cynical

21. The passage suggests that, compared to employees of companies that offer unconditional tuition reimbursement, employees of companies that do not offer this benefit are
  a. less loyal.
  b. more likely to be promoted.
  c. not as smart.
  d. more likely to stay with the company.

22. In paragraph two, the word *expendable* most nearly means
  a. expensive.
  b. flexible.
  c. replaceable.
  d. extraneous.

23. The main idea of the passage is that
  a. companies should reimburse employees for work-related courses.
  b. both companies and employees would benefit from unconditional tuition reimbursement.
  c. companies should require their employees to take college courses.
  d. by insisting on a college degree, companies will be better able to fill vacancies from within.

Read each question carefully and select the word that is the synonym or antonym for the word provided.

24. An antonym for *disperse* is
  a. gather.
  b. agree.
  c. praise.
  d. satisfy.

25. A synonym for *eccentric* is
  a. normal.
  b. frugal.
  c. peculiar.
  d. selective.

26. A synonym for *commendable* is
  a. admirable.
  b. accountable.
  c. irresponsible.
  d. noticeable.

27. An antonym for *prevarication* is
   a. accolade.
   b. veracity.
   c. deprecation.
   d. mendacity.

28. An antonym for *mirth* is
   a. pallor.
   b. solemnity.
   c. penury.
   d. lethargy.

29. A synonym for *domain* is
   a. entrance.
   b. rebellion.
   c. formation.
   d. territory.

30. An antonym for *orient* is
   a. confuse.
   b. arouse.
   c. deter.
   d. simplify.

Answer each of the following grammar and usage questions.

31. Which of the following sentences uses capitalization correctly?
   a. Last Thursday, my Mother, my Aunt Barbara, and I went to the museum to see an exhibit of African art.
   b. Last Thursday, my mother, my aunt Barbara, and I went to the museum to see an exhibit of African art.
   c. Last Thursday, my mother, my aunt Barbara, and I went to the Museum to see an exhibit of African art.
   d. Last Thursday, my mother, my aunt Barbara, and I went to the museum to see an exhibit of African Art.

32. Which of the following sentences uses periods correctly?
   a. Dr Harrison will speak at the hotel in Chicago, Ill, on thurs at 3:00 P.M.
   b. Dr. Harrison will speak at the hotel in Chicago, Ill, on Thurs at 3:00 PM.
   c. Dr Harrison will speak at the hotel in Chicago, Ill, on Thurs. at 3:00 P.M.
   d. Dr. Harrison will speak at the hotel in Chicago, Ill., on Thurs. at 3:00 P.M.

33. Which of the following sentences is NOT a complete sentence?

    a. Hearing the thunder, the lifeguard ordered us out of the water.

    b. Turn off the lights.

    c. Sunday afternoon spent reading and playing computer games.

    d. I was surprised to see that my neighbor had written a letter to the editor.

34. Which of the following sentences is a complete sentence?

    a. The newspapers are supposed to be delivered by 7:00, but I am usually finished before 6:45.

    b. I called the delivery service this morning, they told me the shipment would arrive on time.

    c. Look in the closet you should find it there.

    d. I was the first to sign the petition Harry was the second.

35. Which of the following sentences uses the correct verb form?

    a. Margaret brang a cake so that everyone in the office could help celebrate her birthday.

    b. Margaret brought a cake so that everyone in the office could help celebrate her birthday.

    c. Margaret bring a cake so that everyone in the office could help celebrate her birthday.

    d. Margaret had brung a cake so that everyone in the office could help celebrate her birthday.

36. Which of the following sentences shows subject/verb agreement?

    a. Neither of the dogs have been to obedience training.

    b. Neither of the dogs were to obedience training.

    c. Neither of the dogs is been to obedience training.

    d. Neither of the dogs has been to obedience training.

37. Which of the following sentences shows subject/verb agreement?

    a. One of the customers have complained about poor service.

    b. Neither of the customers have complained about poor service.

    c. Each of the customers have complained about poor service.

    d. Some of the customers have complained about poor service.

38. Which of the following sentences uses the italicized pronoun incorrectly?

    a. Alicia and *me* want to spend Saturday at Six Flags Amusement Park.

    b. Either Sam or William will bring *his* CD player to the party.

    c. She and *I* will work together on the project.

    d. Why won't you let *her* come with us?

39. Which of the following sentences uses pronouns correctly?
  a. Four band members and *me* were chosen to attend the state competition; one of *we* will do the driving.
  b. Four band members and *me* were chosen to attend the state competition; one of *us* will do the driving.
  c. Four band members and *I* were chosen to attend the state competition; one of *we* will do the driving.
  d. Four band members and *I* were chosen to attend the state competition; one of *us* will do the driving.

Choose the misspelled word in the questions below. If there are no mistakes, select choice d.

40. a. phenomonal
  b. emulate
  c. misconception
  d. no mistakes

41. a. mischief
  b. temperture
  c. loveable
  d. no mistakes

42. a. stadium
  b. competitor
  c. atheletic
  d. no mistakes

43. a. dictionary
  b. auditorium
  c. biology
  d. no mistakes

44. a. geometry
  b. perimeter
  c. circumferance
  d. no mistakes

45. a. general
  b. corporal
  c. lieutenant
  d. no mistakes

Choose the correctly spelled word for the following sentences.

46. Do you think I should run for a seat on the city _____?
   a. counsel
   b. council

47. The amount for the carpet was a _____ price.
   a. fair
   b. fare

48. This problem is _____ complex.
   a. two
   b. to
   c. too

49. My grandmother is an _____ historian.
   a. imminent
   b. immanent
   c. eminent

50. _____ only four o'clock in the afternoon.
   a. It's
   b. Its

ANSWERS

1. **d.** To be *recalcitrant* is to be stubbornly resistant.
2. **c.** To have *rapport* is to have mutual trust and emotional affinity.
3. **d.** A *fervent* voice is one that has great emotion or zest.
4. **b.** *Cryptic* means mysterious, hidden, or enigmatic.
5. **a.** *Copious* means plentiful or abundant.
6. **b.** A *deferment* is a delay.
7. **b.** *Exempt* means to be excused from a rule or obligation.
8. **a.** That which is *scintillating* is brilliant or sparkling.
9. **c.** *Frivolous* means not worthy of serious attention; of little importance.
10. **a.** *Subsequent* means following a specified thing in order or succession.
11. **d.** *Accordance* means in agreement or harmony.
12. **b.** *Succulents* are plants that have leaves specifically for storing water.
13. **a.** *Burgeoning* means emerging or new growth.
14. **c.** *Finesse* is skill, tact, and cleverness.
15. **b.** *Judicious* means to use or show good judgment; to be wise or sensible.
16. **b.** The idea that employees will become more valuable if they take courses is stated in the fourth paragraph: "the employer will have had a more sophisticated, more intelligent, and therefore more valuable and productive employee."
17. **c.** This statement describes the many positions that companies can take when considering reimbursement for educational classes. This statement could be verified, as fact, by surveying companies to find out their tuition reimbursement policies.
18. **d.** The writer of this passage states an opinion: "A company that reimburses employees for all college credit courses—whether job related or not—offers a service not only to the employees but to the entire company." The writer then proceeds to give reasons to persuade the reader of the validity of this statement.
19. **a.** By using a word associated with education, the writer is able to reinforce the importance of education and tuition reimbursement.
20. **c.** The passage is optimistic and describes only positive effects of unconditional reimbursement; there are virtually no negative words.
21. **a.** If employees of companies that offer unconditional tuition reimbursement are more loyal to their companies (see the second and third paragraphs), it follows that other employees will be less loyal because their company is not showing enough dedication to their betterment.
22. **c.** *Expendable* means *replaceable*. The writer uses the word immediately after saying that job security is a thing of the past. This clue tells you that workers do not feel they are important or valuable to a company that can fire them on a moment's notice.
23. **b.** This main idea is explicitly stated in the last sentence of the first paragraph and again at the end of the passage.
24. **a.** *Disperse* means to scatter; to *gather* means to collect in one place.

25. **c.** An *eccentric* person is considered to be odd, unusual, eccentric, or *peculiar*.

26. **a.** Both *commendable* and *admirable* mean worthy, qualified, or desirable.

27. **b.** *Prevarication* is an evasion of the truth; *veracity* means truthfulness.

28. **b.** *Mirth* means merriment; *solemnity* means seriousness.

29. **d.** A *domain* is an area governed by a ruler; a *territory* is an area for which someone is responsible.

30. **a.** To *orient* means to adjust, become familiar; to *confuse* means to bewilder.

31. **b.** Every proper noun and adjective in this sentence is correctly capitalized.

32. **d.** Periods are placed after Dr., Ill., Thurs., and P.M.

33. **c.** This is a sentence fragment and is missing the helping verb *was* that would make it a complete sentence.

34. **a.** Choice **a** is the only complete sentence. Choices **b**, **c**, and **d** are run-on sentences.

35. **b.** This sentence is in the past tense and uses the verb *brought*.

36. **d.** *Neither* is singular as is *has been*.

37. **d.** *Some* is plural as is *have complained*.

38. **a.** *Alicia and I* is the subject of the sentence, therefore the subjective pronoun *I* has to be used to make the sentence correct.

39. **d.** *Four band members and I* is the subject of the sentence; the subjective pronoun *I* is correct. *Us* is the object of the preposition; the objective pronoun *us* is correct.

40. **a.** The correct spelling is *phenomenal*.

41. **b.** The correct spelling is *temperature*.

42. **c.** The correct spelling is *athletic*.

43. **d.** no mistakes

44. **c.** The correct spelling is *circumference*.

45. **d.** no mistakes

46. **b.** The correct spelling is *council*.

47. **a.** The correct spelling is *fair*.

48. **c.** The correct spelling is *too*.

49. **c.** The correct spelling is *eminent*.

50. **a.** The correct spelling is *It's*.

Glossary of Vocabulary Terms

active voice: when the subject is performing the action (as opposed to *passive voice*)

agreement: the state of being balanced in number (e.g., singular subjects and singular verbs; plural antecedents and plural pronouns)

antecedent: the noun that is replaced by a pronoun

cause: a person or thing that makes something happen

clause: a group of words containing a subject and predicate

comparative: the adjective form showing the greater degree in quality or quantity, formed by adding *–er* (e.g., *happier*)

comparison: showing how two ideas or items are similar

complex sentence: a sentence with at least one dependent and one independent clause

compound sentence: a sentence with at least two independent clauses

conjunctive adverb: a word or phrase that often works with a semi-colon to connect two independent clauses and show the relationship to one another (e.g., *however, therefore, likewise*)

contraction: a word that uses an apostrophe to show that a letter or letters have been omitted (e.g., *can't*)

contrast: showing how two ideas or items are different

coordinating: conjunction one of seven words—*and, but, for, nor, or, so, yet*—that serve to connect two independent clauses

dependent clause: a clause that has a subordinating conjunction and expresses an incomplete thought

direct object: the person or thing that receives the action of the sentence

fragment: an incomplete sentence (may or may not have a subject and predicate)

gerund: the *noun* form of a verb, created by adding *–ing* to the verb base

helping verb: (auxiliary verb) verbs that help indicate exactly when an action will take place, is taking place, did take place, should take place, might take place, etc.

homophone: a word that sounds exactly like another word but has a different spelling and meaning (e.g., *bare, bear*)

independent clause: a clause that expresses a complete thought and can stand on its own

indirect object: the person or thing that receives the direct object

infinitive: the base form of a verb plus the word *to* (e.g., *to go*)

intransitive verb: a verb that does not take an object (the subject performs the action on him/her/itself)

mechanics: the rules governing punctuation, capitalization, and spelling

modifier: a word or phrase that describes or qualifies a person, place, thing, or action

parallel structure: a series of words, phrases, or clauses that all follow the same grammatical pattern

participial phrase: the *adjective* form of a verb, created by adding *–ing* to the verb base

passive voice: when the subject of the sentence is being acted upon (passively "receives" the action)

past participle: the verb form expressing what happened in the past, formed by a past tense helping verb + the simple past tense form of the verb

phrase: a group of words that do not contain both a subject and a predicate

predicate: the part of the sentence that tells us what the subject is or does

present participle: the verb form expressing what is happening now, formed by a present tense helping verb and *–ing*

proper noun: a noun that identifies a specific person, place, or thing, such as *Elm Street*

redundancy: the unnecessary repetition of words or ideas

run-on: a sentence that has two or more independent clauses without the proper punctuation or connecting words (e.g., *subordinating conjunction*) between them

style: the manner in which something is done; in writing, the combination of a writer's word choice, sentence structure, tone, level of formality, and level of detail

subject: the person, place, or thing that performs the action of the sentence

subjunctive: the verb form that indicates something that is wished for or contrary to fact

subordinating conjunction: a word or phrase that introduces an adverb clause, making the clause dependent and showing its relationship to another (usually independent) clause (e.g. *because, since, while*)

superlative: the adjective form showing the greatest degree in quality or quantity, formed by adding –*est* (e.g., *happiest*)

transition: a word or phrase used to move from one idea to the next and show the relationship between those ideas (e.g., *however, next, in contrast*)

transitive verb: a verb that takes an object (someone or something "receives" the action of the verb)

usage: the rules that govern the form of the words we use and how we string words together in sentences